the series on school reform

Patricia A. Wasley   Ann Lieberman   Joseph P. McDonald
Bank Street College of Education   NCREST   New York University

SERIES EDITORS

This series also incorporates earlier titles in the Professional Development and Practice Series

TEACHERS—
Transforming
Their World
and
Their Work

◆

ANN LIEBERMAN AND LYNNE MILLER

Teachers College
Columbia University
New York and London

Association for Supervision
and Curriculum Development
Alexandria, Virginia

Published by **TEACHERS COLLEGE PRESS**
Teachers College Press, 1234 Amsterdam Avenue, New York, NY 10027
Orders: 1-800-575-6566
Editorial offices: 212-678-3929 http://tc-press.tc.columbia.edu

in conjunction with
Association for Supervision and Curriculum Development
1703 N. Beauregard Street • Alexandria, VA 22311-1714 USA
Telephone: 1-800-933-2723 or 703-578-9600 • Fax 703-575-5400
Web site http://www.ascd.org • E-mail: member@ascd.org
ASCD ISBN 1-87120-352-9 ASCD Stock No. 199217   s3/99

Library of Congress Cataloging-in-Publication Data

Lieberman, Ann.

    Teachers—transforming their world and their work / Ann
Lieberman and Lynne Miller.
      p.   cm. — (The series on school reform)
    Includes bibliographical references and index.
    ISBN 0-8077-3858-1 (paper : alk. paper)
    1. Teaching—United States. 2. Public schools—United States.
3. Teacher effectiveness—United States. 4. Educational change—
United States.   I. Miller, Lynne, 1945–   II. Title.   III. Series.
LB1025.3 .L547 1999
371.102'0973—dc21   99-13653

ISBN 0-8077-3858-1 (paper)

Printed on acid-free paper

Manufactured in the United States of America

06 05 04 03 02 01 00 99   8 7 6 5 4 3 2 1

We dedicate this book to the present generation of students,
especially our children and grandchildren:
Daniel, Elizabeth, Katy, Jennie, Jeannie, Peter, and Aaron,

and

to the teachers who struggle daily
to transform their world and their work
so that ALL children can learn

CONTENTS

◆

ACKNOWLEDGMENTS

◆

LIKE THE teachers and principals we write about in this book, we approach our work with hope and commitment. Mindful of its complexity and challenge, we are willing to learn as we go along. And we realize that our learning is always informed by the learning of others. We want to thank our many public school colleagues who have allowed us to document their thoughts and their actions. We are especially in debt to the teachers and administrators who belong to the Southern Maine Partnership; they consistently demonstrated that schools can be places where children and adults can learn and thrive. Thanks are also in order to educators in New York and California who steadfastly reminded us that classroom and school practice is the key to increased student achievement. Thanks also to our university colleagues and the people connected to the National Center for Restructuring Education, Schools, and Teaching at Teachers College, Columbia University. Denise Brown worked conscientiously, and under rushed conditions, to complete the preparation of our manuscript; we are grateful for her talent, patience, and skill.

As always, we owe a special thanks to our husbands, Ernie Lieberman and Larry Simon. They cleared the table when we needed space to work, tended to children and grandchildren when we were at the keyboard, and listened to us when we complained about the book and about each other. They continue to be our most ardent advocates and our most honest critics.

Finally, we have to acknowledge our unique and wonderful collaboration. For twenty years, we have been able to think together and write together about things that matter. We share our stories, our ideas, and our questions. We offer support and critique in equal measure, always acknowledging what we know and don't know. We continue to be each other's best teacher, student, and friend.

INTRODUCTION

◆

If there is no struggle, there is no progress. Those who profess to favor freedom and yet deprecate agitation . . . want crops without plowing up the ground. They want rain without thunder and lightning. They want the ocean without the awful roar of its many waters.

Frederick Douglass, 1857

THIS IS a book about transforming education, schools, and teaching. But mostly it is about teaching and teachers. We chose this focus because we believe that teachers are at the center of all efforts to improve schools, that without their full participation and leadership, any move to reform education—no matter how well intentioned or ambitious—is doomed to failure. This volume follows on our earlier work, *Teachers: Their World and Their Work* (1984), in which we sought to gain understandings about the social realities of teaching from the teacher's perspective. Our hunch then was that embedded in these understandings were the starting points for school regeneration and teacher growth and development. We wanted schools to change, but we realized that change would be slow and that, to be successful, it had to be grounded in the lived experiences and professional knowledge of teachers.

Now, 15 years later, many schools and the teachers who work in them are being challenged to achieve more ambitious and far-reaching goals than we would have imagined a decade ago. As we approach the 21st century, we are in the midst of a standards-based reform movement that promotes high levels of achievement for all students—not just the top 20%. This vision of education is a direct challenge to many of the principles and practices of public education as we know it. If we are to ensure that all students have access to high quality schooling, then we need to rethink and redesign schools.

In the 1980s and 1990s a plethora of reports has decried the state of American public education. In 1983, the National Commission on Excellence in Education declared in *A Nation at Risk* that nothing short of a fundamental rethinking of the school will suffice to prepare Americans for the 21st century. Three years later, the Carnegie Report on Teaching (Task Force on Teaching as a Profession, 1986) called for the professionalization of teaching and cited the need for teacher leadership at the forefront of any reform movement. Many others joined the chorus, recommending a shift from bureaucratic, top-down school structures to ones that are oriented toward the making of a real profession (Clark & Meloy, 1990; Darling-Hammond, 1990). More recently, the National Commission on Teaching and America's Future (1996) published a comprehensive blueprint for change that provides for the preparation of teachers and for their continuous learning throughout their careers. These reports have shown us the many contexts in which teaching and learning occur. They have helped us understand schools and their problems as well as the conditions necessary to bring about change.

Too often, discussions about school change take place in the rarified atmospheres of universities, foundations, and business round tables, where talking about schools is abstract and far removed from the realities of both teaching and schools. In this book, we hope to enrich the current dialogue and to bring the reader closer to these realities by focusing on the constraints as well as the possibilities that are embedded in practice. Our views grow out of our continuous work and involvement in reforming schools from several perspectives: as writers, editors, and critical readers of the literature on school reform and change, and as observers, researchers, and participants in school reform networks and state and local initiatives. We depend on observations and structured interviews and informal conversations in Maine, New York, and California and on the insights and wisdom gathered from educators across the country with whom we have met during the past decade and a half. The words and experiences of these seasoned teachers and administrators are the backbone of this book.

Since the publication of our first book, we have witnessed and participated in many changes in public education. Ann Lieberman has worked with five reform networks and reform projects from California to New York. She recently retired from Teachers College, Columbia University, where she served as Professor of Curriculum and Teaching and also co-directed the National Center for Restructuring Education, Schools, and Teaching. She is currently Visiting Professor at Stanford University and Senior Scholar at the Carnegie Foundation for the Advancement of Teaching. Lynne Miller has completed 11 years as Professor of Educational Leadership at the University of Southern Maine and Director of the Southern Maine Partnership. The Partnership is a school/university collaboration with its roots in "the simultaneous renewal" of individuals and institutions, of schools and the education of teachers (Goodlad, 1988). She has been active in school reform in Maine and across the country, and she served as a member of the National Commission on Teaching and America's Future. We both continue to teach, and we consider this our true vocation.

We have experienced change in our personal lives as well. Ann has become a grandmother five times over, and Lynne has become the mother of two children (now both in middle school). Having school-age children so close at hand has made our work more immediate and urgent. We are writing this book for the present generation of children and the teachers who teach them. We write with hope, passion, and commitment—firm in our belief that teachers can transform their work and, in so doing, transform the world that children experience in school.

TEACHERS—
Transforming
Their World
and
Their Work

TRANSFORMING SCHOOLING AND TEACHING
What Matters and What Works

Schools are social institutions that need to provide mechanisms for exchanging ideas and defining collective visions, always open to negotiating and redefining these visions according to the needs of the community.

John Dewey, 1916

FOR THE PAST decade and a half, a wide array of groups—academics, governors, foundations, teacher unions, national commissions, professional associations, innovative school leaders, state departments of education, and parent and community organizations—have been hard at work developing models and methods for improving schools. Some of these groups have focused on the processes of schooling, others on its outcomes; still others have looked at the structures of public schools or have concentrated on the teaching force and how to improve it. We believe that the transformation of schooling and the transformation of teaching are interconnected. We cannot reform schools without reforming teaching, and we cannot reform teaching without reforming schools.

What we are about is developing a new language that describes what is possible. Phillip Schlechty (1990) calls this "invention"—the invention of new ways of thinking and of organizing so that students can be reached more effectively. Such invention cannot be a collection of sporadic and disjointed efforts. Rather, it is as "steady work" that is inclusive and broad-based and grounded in the day-to-day realities of school life (Elmore & McLaughlin, 1988).

Efforts to change schools and teaching focus on issues and visions that cannot be mandated, despite the best intentions of policy makers.

1

Nor are they likely to spring up on their own. Reform is collectively created within a supportive environment that encourages people to learn about and to work through the change process. Prescriptions rarely help, but neither do laissez-faire approaches. Effective approaches to change might include establishing goals based on some significant values, standards, or beliefs; outlining the procedural means to accomplish these goals; and putting in place an organizational structure that provides continuous support and learning. But these conditions are not easily created. Although everyone builds on ideas that are created by others, variation rather than standardization is the norm.

APPROACHES TO SCHOOL CHANGE

We have found it helpful to categorize reform in the schools as either procedural or principled. While these categories are not mutually exclusive, we have found one or the other to be dominant when a given school and its faculty embrace change. We believe that both are needed to create and sustain fundamental shifts in the process of schooling and teaching.

Procedural Approaches

In one of the first legislative actions for school reform in the mid 1980s, the state of Washington allowed selected schools to restructure themselves. The legislation emphasized collaboration and rigorous evaluation of the reform efforts and provided procedures for waiving state regulations if they impeded progress. In Maine in the early 1980s, the state awarded small grants to 10 schools to support their restructuring efforts. Each school that applied for a grant had to present a vision for its restructuring project, demonstrate a willingness to make restructuring a collaborative effort, and provide some means of assessing the outcome. These two examples represent a procedural approach to change at the state level.

The procedural approach can also be seen at the district level. In Dade County, Florida, the school district offered pilot schools the opportunity to create school-level committees, each of which was empowered to chart a course for change in a given area. In New York City, the Chancellor tied the flexible use of Chapter 1 funds to a negotiated union agreement for a "school-based option" that allows schools to restructure when 75% of the teachers and the building principal agree on a focus that seems likely to better meet the needs of all students.

In Chicago, local school councils were organized by state legislation to oversee an ambitious and controversial school change effort.

These early efforts at restructuring schools are examples of procedures that were put in place to provide both supports and boundaries for the work. Some procedures gave school personnel the organizational means for rethinking their schools, such as school-level committees. Other procedures offered new incentives for rethinking schools, such as more staff development or increased planning time for teachers. Still other procedures provided structures for—and encouraged teachers to participate more actively in—decision making related to the curriculum, instruction, and organization of the school.

Principled Approaches

Other improvement efforts rely more on values or principles than on procedures. These efforts are rarely initiated at the state level. They tend to evolve outside of traditional educational structures, and they articulate values at a level of generality that allows for—indeed, encourages—individual variation. For example, the Coalition of Essential Schools, spearheaded by Ted Sizer (Houston, 1988), works to transform secondary schools by stressing 10 core principles to which all member schools subscribe. Among these principles are personalizing learning, helping adolescents learn to use their minds well, establishing school goals that apply to all students, and helping students achieve mastery of a limited number of essential skills and areas of knowledge. Ernest Boyer (1991) has done similar work for elementary schools in his description of a framework that describes the "Basic School." Member schools agree to work on a framework that involves the school as a community and includes a coherent curriculum, a climate that encourages learning, and a commitment to character.

Schlechty (1988), in his original work in Louisville, Kentucky, also offered a set of principles in the form of standards that grew from beliefs about the need for visionary leadership in the pursuit of equity and excellence. Schlechty's standards include having a shared vision, relying on participatory decision-making, and focusing on outcomes. He helped develop new metaphors to guide the work, such as "the student as worker," "the teacher as leader," and "the principal as leader of leaders." Likewise, John Goodlad (1984), in forming the National Network for Educational Renewal, established a clear agenda and proposed a set of principles to change simultaneously teacher education and public schools. Here again, the focus is on a core of values that fixes the boundaries for the work but provides broad opportunities for creating a variety of means to get there.

While each of these reform efforts allows for variations that stem from different contexts, each refuses to compromise on its core beliefs and preferred practices. Each effort also helps its participating schools to identify with ideas larger than the individual, the classroom, the school, or the community. When there is a set of guiding principles, people can form a common language for conversation and common understandings to motivate action.

BUILDING BLOCKS FOR TRANSFORMING SCHOOLING AND TEACHING

When we think about changing schools and teaching, we find it helpful to identify the building blocks that underlie any of these efforts. These building blocks combine procedures and principles and include the following:

Rethinking Curriculum and Instruction to Improve Quality and Promote Equality

This is the cornerstone of whole-school change; it implies a systemic questioning of all current instructional practices and a willingness to modify—even, if necessary, to eliminate—basic tenets that educators have traditionally held about what learning is and how it can be promoted for all students. Teachers question practices such as tracking, sorting children by age into grade levels, and departmentalizing learning into disparate academic disciplines. They seek new ways to define and evaluate student achievement as well as new criteria by which to define an educated person.

Rethinking the Structure of the School

This building block focuses on school operations and is based on the belief that changes in instructional practices will require a change in how schools are organized and administered. Specifically, the role of the teacher is targeted for reexamination and redefinition. Opportunities for ongoing teacher learning and participation are central here. Such constructs as coaching, mentoring, task groups, teacher leadership, school-based management, and participatory decision-making fall into this category. Recent support for charter schools also demonstrates a concern for how schools are organized.

Adopting a Two-Pronged Focus: Students and Teachers

Neither an exclusive focus on students nor an exclusive focus on teachers leads to comprehensive change in the schools. The two goals of creating a rich learning environment for students and a professionally supportive environment for teachers must go hand-in-hand, and keeping both goals alive has emerged as a crucial element in successful school restructuring. School-based management and new decision-making structures are not ends in themselves; they are means to achieving more effective environments for learning and teaching. Changes in instructional practices do not take hold in schools that infantilize teachers and push them into patterns of defensiveness and conservatism. Standards for students make no sense if they are not accompanied by standards for teachers. Schools that attend to one side of the student/teacher equation without acknowledging the other are schools in which change is more often illusory than real, more espoused than enacted.

Making Connections Outside the School

School faculties that are in the process of reforming themselves and their institutions have found it important to form alliances among themselves and with teachers from other schools so they can explore possibilities and exchange ideas, insights, and experiences. Regional, state, and national coalitions, partnerships, and reform networks provide the mechanisms for sharing information and for developing a common language and a collective view of reform work. Some examples include the National Writing Project, the Bay Area School Reform Collaborative, the League of Professionals Schools, the Southern Maine Partnership, and the Coalition of Essential Schools. In addition to providing a common language and opportunities for sharing information, outside groups offer support for the difficult work taking place inside schools and the necessary connections to outside knowledge.

Encouraging Increased Participation by Parents and the Community

For too long, parents have been left out of the debates on school reform. Now, however, because schools are moving far beyond mere "fiddling" with programs and procedures, they are involving the communities they serve in that process. Such developments as the Chicago plan for school reorganization, James Comer's work with parents and school reform, and Henry Levin's "Accelerated Schools" demonstrate the growing importance and positive effect of parent and citizen involvement in school affairs. In contrast, the recent passage of a bill in California that limits staff development for teachers to the summer and before school, SB-1274, shows what can happen when parents and other citizens are not included in conversations about reform efforts. When there is no community involvement, rumor, gossip, and lack of information can take on an ideological stance and replace knowledge about the necessity for continuous opportunities for teacher growth and development. (See Figure 1.1 for a summary of the building blocks.)

ENDURING TENSIONS

We believe that the approaches and the building blocks that we have identified represent the realities of change in public schools. It is crucial to remember that the ultimate goal of change is to make schooling better for all children. Procedures are essential, but they are empty when they do not support basic principles and deeply held values about learning and teaching. Principles are important, but they lose their value when they do not have procedures to support them. The building blocks are not ends in themselves but a means to a richer and more engaging education for the young and a richer and more rewarding working and learning environment for the adults as well.

It is common in discussions about school change to forget that efforts to reform schools and teaching are not new. They have a long history. The issues and concerns that we are dealing with today represent what we consider "enduring tensions" that have existed in American education since the end of the nineteenth century. But now we are seeing them differently. Such forces as the growth of technology, changing social conditions in our country, an increasingly diverse population in the schools, and the emergence of a global economy have cast these tensions in a new light (Banks, 1992; Delpit, 1995; Garcia, 1991). To our mind, they are best understood as tensions involving (1) the purpose of education, (2) the content of the curriculum, (3) the social contract of schooling, and (4) the connection between schools and the larger community.

FIGURE 1.1
BUILDING BLOCKS FOR TRANSFORMING
SCHOOLS AND TEACHING

- ◆ Rethinking curriculum and instruction to improve quality and promote equality
- ◆ Rethinking the structure of the school
- ◆ Adopting a two-pronged focus: students and teachers
- ◆ Making connections outside the school
- ◆ Encouraging increased participation by parents and the community

---

The Purpose of Education

For most of the century there has been considerable debate about the aims and ends of education (see, for example, Dewey, 1929/1988, and Whitehead, 1929). The tension between "learning to earn" and learning for its own sake can be traced to 1917, when the U.S. Bureau of Education, in a published report, tied the money value of education to the value of the marketplace. Another way to view this tension is between education for work and education for democracy. Traditionally, educators have endorsed both ends, failing to acknowledge that this stand represents a confusion of goals and an ambiguity about purpose. As Henry Levin (1991) has pointed out, life in the workplace and life in a democracy require different values, attributes, and dispositions. Work emphasizes property and ownership; citizenship values individual rights. Work often limits freedom of expression and freedom of association; citizenship protects these freedoms. Workers follow leaders whom they do not elect; citizens vote to choose who will lead them. This tension remains a powerful one in the current move to transform schools. Are we striving to produce better quality workers? To develop informed citizens for our fragile democracy? To prepare people for the technologies of the 21st century? To develop minds and intelligences? To insure access for all students? To do all of these things?

The Content of the Curriculum

The content of the curriculum has been equally disputed over the past century, having been framed by the differing perspectives of John Dewey and Edward Lee Thorndike. Dewey's commitment to the use of experience in education and the development of an instructional environment that supports discovery and connections has long been juxtaposed to Thorndike's behaviorist approach that views learning as a process of directly giving knowledge and seeking its responses. There are several contemporary versions of this debate. These include the dispute in reading between phonics and whole language and the dispute in mathematics between computation and problem solving. Added to this debate is the unresolved issue of what specific body of knowledge should be taught. The question of what is worth knowing has its roots in the common school movement. It was revisited during the industrial revolution and again during the two world wars, and it continues to come up today in discussions of school reform. Is there a canon that determines cultural literacy? Is education always personal and individual? What is more important, content or process? Is the curriculum a sequenced set of activities prepared in advance, or an emergent response to important questions? Or is it the search for a combination of all of these?

The Social Contract

By "social contract" we mean the tacit agreement that schools have with their publics about who shall be educated and to what level. Public schools in the United States were never designed to educate everyone. Considering that the high school graduate rate has gone from only 8% in 1908 to 50% in 1950 and 82% in 1997, it is fair to say that the social contract has changed radically. Also, the social contract has not been equitable. Historically, schools have practiced a kind of educational triage, providing high quality programs of study for some, adequate programs for others, and substandard or incomplete programs for the rest. Yet the rhetoric of public education has long promised another reality—an educated work force and citizenry, access to opportunity based on merit and hard work, and a free and equal education for all. Educators involved in the current reform and standards movement are heirs to this debate about the desirability and practicality of educating everyone. Is there a set of high standards to which all students can aspire? Can schools ensure that all student learn to think, reason, and manipulate knowledge? How, and in what ways, can schools be held accountable for the success of all students?

School and Community

Finally, there is the tension between the school and the larger community. Do schools operate as separate institutions dedicated exclu-

---

FIGURE 1.2

ENDURING TENSIONS IN SCHOOLING
AND TEACHING

- ◆ The purpose of education
- ◆ The content of the curriculum
- ◆ The social contract
- ◆ School and community

---

sively to academics and matters of the intellect, or do they respond to the needs and values of the communities that surround them? Do schools complement families, or do they supplant them? These are contemporary questions, but they are not new. Since the late 19th century, when schools took on the task of socializing—as well as educating—large immigrant populations, there has been disagreement about where schools stand as part of the larger social order. What should the relationship be between parents and teachers, between school and home? Are schools social service agencies as well as educational institutions? Where are lines drawn? Where are boundaries crossed in the interest of children?

The teachers who are the focus of this book are thoughtfully seeking resolutions to these enduring tensions (see Figure 1.2). They have embraced what we and others call "learner-centered" beliefs and practices. They focus their efforts on schoolwork, teacher work, and community. These are the things that matter most.

Schoolwork is the work that students do in school. In schools engaged in restructuring, schoolwork is based on understandings developed over time about how people construct and use knowledge. The teachers in these schools develop complementary conceptions of learning and teaching. Recent findings in cognitive research, together with Dewey's earlier conception of education, have helped define learning as the assimilation of new information (Brown, 1994; Dewey, 1916/1980; Resnick, 1987; Schaps, Watson & Lewis, 1996). This view of learning assumes that students bring mental maps with them when they enter school. Each map is developed from the student's prior experience, dispositions, and perspectives. According to this view, students use concepts they already have to screen and interpret new knowledge. Thus schoolwork becomes work that is complex, layered, and open to revision and improvement. Mastery of basic skills in literacy and numeracy remains important, but these skills are taught, not as ends in themselves, but as part of a larger context of learning and understanding.

Teachers in schools that are transforming themselves see teacher work mainly as helping students construct their own knowledge rather than as only transmitting knowledge to students. They design and promote high quality schoolwork by focusing on student perspectives and accepting the responsibility and challenge of joining interest, content, and strategy. Teachers work in different ways in different schools— with their students, with one another, and with parents and the community. They assume responsibility and accept accountability for their students' learning and as well as their own. And they take as their charge the education of all students to high levels of achievement.

Community encompasses the relationships that occur day-to-day. It involves teachers, students, families, neighborhoods, and beyond. It is built around shared experiences involving common struggles, successes, and failures. It is sustained by structures that promote dialogue about students, learning, teaching, curriculum, expectations, and results (Lieberman & McLaughlin, 1992; McLaughlin & Talbert, 1993).

WHAT WORKS IN TRANSFORMING SCHOOLS

The transformation of schooling and teaching is supported by a set of norms, values, and ways of doing business that promote positive changes in schoolwork, teacher work, and the community. Some strategies are more successful than others in reaching this end. They include combining content and process, attending to the needs of both teachers and students, and balancing action and reflection.

Combining Content and Process

Finding a starting point for changing is a common problem. Some school staffs start by changing grouping practices (such as mixing ages or creating teams), moving toward cooperative learning, and adopting different learning styles. Others change the schedule to allow for planning or teaching together. Some teachers might use the time together to plan interdisciplinary work, write small units, or develop grade-level or department standards and assessments. Others might start by developing a literacy program that will serve all students. There is no one right starting point in building a new vision for a school. A strong core of teachers is as likely as a strong principal to initiate the vision-building process. District-level initiatives, such as that in District 2 of New York City (Elmore, 1996), may encourage schools to focus on particular areas and grant them the freedom to be innovative. Statewide initiatives may encourage individual school staffs to "think big" about student success and how to achieve it. The local teacher union may encourage restructuring as a major mode of school reform and support local collaborations between schools, colleges, and universities and other districts.

Many other factors also influence the starting point for a school restructuring effort. These include the source of the initial leadership, the current state of the school, the level of communication that already exists among the faculty members, the level of trust that already exists between the faculty and the principal, the values espoused by district leaders and the degree of support they give to the project, the kinds and amount of support available to teachers, and the formal and informal sources of leadership within the faculty. Whether a school first builds a plan and then mobilizes people around it or first brings a wide array of people together to develop a vision, restructuring a school requires the combined effort of the whole school community. Moving into action always unleashes new and unpredictable forces—some of them frustrating, others exhilarating and energizing.

There are many different scenarios, none of them "right" or "wrong." Both content and process are important and necessary, but how they are interwoven in any given reform effort is hard to predict and difficult to describe. History, context, leadership, staffing, incentives, personal histories—all these factors play a role. A vision without accompanying commitment, support, and structures to foster organizational learning will have no chance of becoming a reality. But a process for restructuring without an accompanying vision will have no place to go. Each school community starts with its own set of conditions and must understand that while content is critical, defining the process for building commitment and fostering continuous learning is equally important.

Attending to the Needs of Both Teachers and Students

If change is to have meaning, it must be related to students and their success in schools; and it must acknowledge the needs and concerns of teachers as they change the way they work. Schoolwork and teacher work often compete for attention in schools that are transforming themselves. Many schools are developing ways to encourage discussion about approaches to teaching and learning while enabling teachers themselves to learn and grow. Such efforts help isolated teachers become part of larger learning communities. Although the focus of school change efforts must be on students and their learning, conditions that enable adults to accomplish this goal are as essential. How a staff chooses to work—and on what—has to do with the individuals involved: how much they trust one another, how willing they are to think "out of the box" in new ways about students, how comfortable they feel in new roles, and how sensitive they are to the ways in which their students experience their school. A team might create an interdisciplinary unit and teach together. Or an entire faculty might focus on making its shared vision a reality and choose a starting point with scheduled times for teachers to work together and learn together.

What makes the move to transforming schooling and teaching different from other change efforts is the basic understanding that it is necessary to create the conditions for teachers to accomplish these new goals. The strong connection between students' learning and teachers' workplace conditions cannot be ignored. In schools that do not find the balance, trouble looms ahead. In schools that focus primarily on teachers' workplace conditions, the outside community often responds, "What does all this have to do with the children?" In schools that focus primarily on students' learning, teachers often feel overwhelmed and under appreciated, and they cease to take part in the restructuring effort. Transforming schooling and teaching is hard work. It demands the development of a new web of relationships throughout the school. After years of exposure to staff development "packages" created by consultants and developers, school-based educators are now starting to concentrate on their own teaching practices. As they do, they are developing a sense of their own worth and what it means to be professionally healthy.

Balancing Action and Reflection

When teachers embark on a new project, they generally devote a great deal of time to defining goals and objectives. But the reality of practice is much messier, much less linear, and decidedly less comfortable. People accept an idea that they may not know much about because they care about the underlying values. But an idea does not become real until people start doing something about enacting the idea. Out of the doing comes more ideas about what needs to be done, what supports are necessary, what knowledge is important,

---

FIGURE 1.3

WHAT WORKS IN TRANSFORMING SCHOOLS

◆ Combining content and process
◆ Attending to the needs of both teachers and students
◆ Balancing action and reflection

---

what difficulties are likely to arise, and what future directions seem appropriate (Weick, 1979).

How people begin to think about and act in their schools, how shared visions come into being, how people learn to take risks, what people read, how people transform their ideas into practice, how ordinary people begin to do extraordinary things—this is the stuff of school change. How much time does it take to build staff cohesion around an idea for restructuring a school? Is it better to start doing something immediately, or first to spend time learning to talk with one another and to make decisions together? Can staff members learn to trust one another while they are engaged in curricular and pedagogical changes?

While schools and teachers approach change in a variety of ways, most experience the process as neither predictable nor orderly but often fitful and pragmatic. Most of us have had little experience with transforming big ideas into workable practices without losing the essence of the ideas. Working through such complicated issues as democracy in the workplace, developing colleagueship, and expanding responsibilities for teachers and students is complex work. And there are no road maps to guide us. Instead, there is uncharted territory open to exploration and invention. But in the process of this invention, we are learning that to transform school (see Figure 1.3), we must also transform teaching.

VIEWS FROM PRACTICE

What does the kind of transformation we have been talking about look like in practice? How is it initiated and extended in actual schools and classrooms? Here we present profiles of four schools in the midst of change. These views from practice show the kinds of changes teachers are making in their schools and how they are making them. We return to these four schools later in the book when we investigate other areas of the change process.

New Orchard Elementary School

A rural elementary school serving students in grades K–6, New Orchard has been involved in a process of change for over 10 years. Learning for children and adults is placed at the center of its work. The school is a fully inclusive program, combining students with special needs and other students in both multi-age and traditional grade-level classrooms. Systematic and continuous teacher research has guided instructional practices for over a decade. Since 1996, the school has led teachers to develop schoolwide benchmarks and assessments for students. The results of these assessments are published annually, making New Orchard a leader in developing a local accountability system for student learning. The goal of the school, according to its principal, is to provide students with "a continuous journey, rather than a series of disconnected trips." To that end, the New Orchard staff have taken on the ambitious agenda of involving the entire school district (six schools encompassing seven towns) in a comprehensive assessment and accountability system.

Wright Middle School

An urban middle school serving 520 students in grades 6, 7, and 8, Wright is a multicultural enclave in a city dominated by white ethnic groups. Sixty-five percent of its students are on free or reduced lunch, and 20% are from homes where languages other than English are spoken. The school is divided into houses where teams of teachers spend all day with the same students. The program of study is built around a series of teacher-developed "expeditions." These are interdisciplinary curriculum units that culminate in a major project intended for an audience beyond the teacher. Student work is displayed throughout the building, and descriptors of good writing and the criteria of good work are posted in every classroom. Every year, the school hosts a Demonstration Fair and invites parents and community members to view student work and to engage students in conversations about their work. The fair lasts a full day; it begins at 8:00 a.m. and ends at 8:00 p.m. One team has successfully initiated "looping," moving the entire seventh-grade class into eighth grade with the same team of teachers. Other teams are now moving in that direction. The culture of the school is best captured by the large sculpture of a book that greets every visitor to the school. In bold print that cannot escape notice, the title of the book announces *Great Expectations.*

Aronomink School

Teachers at Aronomink School have resisted the pressure merely to adopt innovations. Instead, they have adapted new approaches to teaching and assessment while maintaining traditions that continue to serve them and their students well. Like New Orchard, the school combines multi-age and traditional classes. Appropriateness and utility, informed by investigation and reflection, guide the work at Aronomink. The school has been a leader in the district in using student exhibitions and portfolios to demonstrate achievement. It also has been a pioneer in designing units that integrate curriculum, instruction, and assessment, and in establishing conferences (at entry, progress, and exit points) involving parents and led by children. Aronomink is best characterized by the sign in front of the building, "Aronomink School, A Center of Inquiry," and the greeting that all visitors encounter:

> Welcome to Aronomink School—a Center of Inquiry. We recognize and respect the individual's talents and strengths. We value the opportunity to create and nurture a climate that promotes human potential.

Stratton High School

A rural high school serving 900 students whose families range from the working poor to the lower echelons of the middle class, Stratton has assessment scores that rival those of wealthier suburban districts. Such achievement has not always been the norm at Stratton. The school has moved from a traditional high school structure to one where all classes (with the exception of seven advanced placement courses) are heterogeneously grouped and where differentiated assessments provide students with the choice to pursue honors grades in a course. Departments have been replaced by learning areas, and departmental heads have been eliminated. Students participate in Socratic seminars as well as regular classes in blocks of 90 minutes each and are required to complete a service project in order to graduate. All students take four years of mathematics and science. Teachers have eliminated "basic" math courses. As a result, all ninth graders take algebra, and all seniors take mathematics beyond algebra and geometry, usually calculus. In science, most seniors are enrolled in physics. In fact, the school has the highest percentage (almost 100%) of seniors in physics and advanced math in the state. Overcrowded and underfunded, Stratton High

School has 19 mobile units. Yet the school maintains a unified culture, best characterized by Sizer's (1984) notion that schools should be mindful places where students are engaged in learning and are able to demonstrate their academic accomplishment.

A Continuous Process

Each of these schools has been engaged in a continuous process of improvement. New Orchard began its process with a teacher research initiative in 1987. Aronomink, that same year, developed a vision to guide its work for the next decade. Wright Middle School adopted the principles of middle-level education in the late 1980s, and Stratton High School began its change effort in 1990.

In all four schools, the process of change has been marked by diligence and perseverance. None of these schools followed a smooth path toward change. Oftentimes they were targeted for criticism in their own districts. Identified as "the jewels in the crown" within a district, the schools received attention they did not seek and approbation they felt they did not deserve. This often led to resentment from colleagues in neighboring schools who felt that their own good work was being ignored. There were criticisms as well from within: teachers, parents, and students often voiced disagreement with the new direction the schools were taking.

These schools had to learn how to strike a balance between content and process, teacher and student needs, and reflection and action. Sometimes the schools pushed forward, but other times they slowed down or backed off. Aronomink and New Orchard consistently maintained low-key approaches, providing continual opportunities for people to come on board. Teachers were invited to investigate new practices and to talk about them. Multi-age classes and inclusion practices were implemented slowly and only after teachers expressed readiness. In contrast, Stratton and Wright took more assertive approaches. Stratton implemented changes that a core of faculty and the principal decided were good for learning in the long run, even though some students and staff did not agree. Despite initial opposition to de-tracking classes from the majority of students and a vocal minority of teachers, the school forged ahead and implemented the changes quickly and efficiently. A recent study of seniors, who were freshmen when the de-tracking policy was initiated, found that students now prefer heterogeneous classes and think they are more effective than the ability grouping they experienced in junior high school.

Similarly, Wright joined the Expeditionary Learning project without the approval of the full staff. The principal and a cadre of supportive teachers took the initiative and attended the first summer experience on a raft in white water. This core group invited the rest of the faculty to join them in the project over the course of the next five years. Now Expeditionary Learning is a signature of the whole school and is practiced, to varying degrees, in all of the teams in the building.

Taken together, these four schools demonstrate how the process of transformation begins and persists. Each school honors the needs of its context; each supports at least one structural change; each learns to deal with conflict; and each brings the whole school staff along in its own way and at its own pace.

THE NEW SOCIAL REALITIES
OF TEACHING

◆ ◆ ◆ ◆ ◆

*In this vision of the teaching life, the teacher believes resolutely in
the transformative power of a community of learners; she takes her
stance among the uncertainties of the daily work with her eyes tuned
to a vision of the world as her students might re-create it someday.
It is not enough to strive for students' individual improvement ... or
for some sense of one's technical competence. One must teach for a
democratic future.*

Joseph P. McDonald, *Teaching:
Making Sense of an Uncertain Craft*

TEACHERS ENGAGED in reform are involved in two enormous projects. They are reinventing school, and they are reinventing themselves. The social realities they face are very different from those they have come to know and understand in the past. When we wrote *Teachers: Their World and Their Work* (Lieberman & Miller, 1984), we identified eight "social system understandings" about teaching that seemed to capture the prevailing mood of schools in the 1970s and 1980s. We used the term "social system understandings" because we wanted to emphasize the interplay between individual teacher experiences and the social context of schools. Our understandings led us to portray teaching as a profession that was personalized and individualistic, where rewards were derived from students in the absence of a viable professional community. We described the uncertainty of the craft, the weak links between teaching and learning, and the underdeveloped knowledge base of the profession. We called attention to the vague and conflicting goals of education that entrapped and immobilized teachers and that made good control more easily acknowledged than good teaching. We wrote about the loneliness of the work and the lack of professional support. We concluded by saying that despite efforts to make a science of teaching, it remained an art forged in isolation and invisible to the world of adults.

MAKING TRANSITIONS

As school staffs reorganize their world and their work, they are transforming the very nature of teaching. The understandings we developed in the past no longer hold true. They need to be replaced by new understandings of the social realities of teaching. These new understandings mark a shift in both perspective and practice. The new realities and how they look from the teacher's perspective is at the core of this chapter and lays the foundation for the rest of the book.

From Individualism to Professional Community

The individualism, isolation, and privatism of traditional schools (Lortie, 1975) lead to conservatism and stasis. Emerging norms of collegiality, openness, and trust among teachers (Little, 1981; McLaughlin & Talbert, 1993; Rosenholtz, 1989), however, help develop more dynamic and responsive school cultures. Working jointly to deal with problems of curriculum and instruction is one way teachers develop these new norms. Teachers come together in teams or as whole school staffs to decide on common goals, develop integrated programs of study, craft shared assessments, or examine student work. There is time set aside for planning together, for teaching together, and for talking together. Peer observation and consultation contribute to a shared professional culture in which risks are encouraged, mistakes acknowledged, and learning scrutinized.

This move to a common culture of teaching does not come easily. At times there are conflicts between the personalized style that the old ways supported and the common culture of teaching that the new way promotes. Teachers struggle to find and maintain their own voices even as they work to develop a collective vision. Having forged a personal style and identity, they question which parts of their individual repertoire are worth keeping and which should be abandoned or enhanced. Teachers want to be part of a collegial culture, but they do not want to lose their individuality to what they fear might become a new form of "groupthink." This apparent tension between the individual and the group can be a healthy tension in schools where such talk is openly acknowledged as legitimate.

From Teaching at the Center to Learning at the Center

The shift from "What do I do as a teacher and transmitter of knowledge?" to "How can I plan with others and alone for what students do as learners?" means that, in effect, student work determines the agenda for teacher work. Teachers do not plan their curriculum from abstract goals or from objectives divorced from the realities of their classrooms. They "plan backwards" from outcomes and assessments of actual students (McDonald, 1991). Planning begins with an examination of student work: samples of writing, problem solving, logical thinking, and creative arts are collected and analyzed as a first step in building designs for learning. Rather than focusing exclusively on how teachers teach (collaborative learning, direct instruction, questioning strategies, and so forth), educators focus as well on how students learn as the basis for teaching. As a result, the curriculum of the school is not constructed a priori. It develops within the context of real classrooms with real students. Often this new curriculum centers on themes, questions, projects, or research designed to give students opportunities to learn and responsibility for their learning. The responsibility of the teacher then is to struggle with the connections between curriculum, school organization, and the personal learning needs of students and to design environments where learning can take place.

From Technical Work to Inquiry

When teachers focus on learning, they see their work in a different light. They stop thinking of teaching as a collection of skills or the mastery of techniques and see it instead as intellectual work that engages them in posing problems and seeking solutions, raising questions and answering them, and creating knowledge and using it. Research, reflection, and systematic inquiry are at the core of teachers' work in schools that are restructuring themselves. Like their students, teachers are engaged in a process of continual learning. They are researchers, meaning makers, and scholars studying the question, How do students learn? The inquiry is genuine, for it is based on real-life concerns that are raised in designing and promoting learning for real students. As this culture develops and teachers inquire more deeply into their practice, they learn to find time and opportunities to talk together about their discoveries.

From Control to Accountability

In traditional practice, teachers expend tremendous energy maintaining order and discipline, to "keep the lid on." Being in control is a much-admired attribute and is often the only way that teachers are judged by their peers. Because one's teaching is private and one's classroom inviolate, there is no other publicly accessible evidence of effectiveness.

In schools that are restructuring, student performance is made public; this makes accountability for student learning more important than accountability for behavior. Instead of working to establish norms of control, teachers work to establish norms of learning. They share a belief that they control the conditions for their students' success in school. The realities of personal life, including family history, family structure, and economic status, are not denied, but neither are they accepted as excuses for students not to learn and perform in school. Each teacher assumes responsibility for creating a classroom where students can master school knowledge at an appropriate pace and with a high degree of challenge. This responsibility for learning does not stop at the classroom door. Because learning is viewed as integrated and cumulative, teachers also hold themselves responsible for the learning of the whole school. They develop mechanisms to promote a collective form of accountability.

From Managed Work to Leadership

When student learning and public performances become the products schools develop, the teaching role changes dramatically. Teachers become more like designers, musical conductors, coaches, and leaders. They turn over the production function of schools to their students, creating a major change in the power relationships between adults and their students. Teachers relinquish "power over" their students in exchange for "power to" effect improved student performance (Sergiovanni, 1987).

Leadership is iterative. In the same way that teachers give up control to enhance student learning, principals and other administrators diffuse power to enhance school development. Teachers gain responsibility for areas traditionally reserved for administrators—instruction, assessment, rules and procedures, and major decision making. In effect, they become leaders, and incorporate these qualities into their teaching role.

From Classroom Concerns to Whole-School Concerns and Beyond

Teachers, in adjusting the boundaries of their work, find that the classroom is, as always, an important venue but not the only one. For as teachers work together to create a professional community, they move from solely individual concerns about *my* classroom and *my* students to concerns about *our* school and *our* students. Accountability for student learning expands from the classroom to the school as all adults assume responsibility for the learning of all students. Teachers begin to think of the culture of the whole school and how to develop and support it. They engage in conversations about what the school stands for, how it should be organized and governed, and how it is fulfilling its mission. They also extend themselves beyond their schools, joining partnerships and networks with other like-minded educators. This helps them to expand their thinking, strengthen their resolve, and commit themselves to higher goals.

From a Weak Knowledge Base to a Broad Knowledge Base

Throughout most of this century the knowledge base about teaching was underdeveloped and lacked the codification common to other professions. That condition has changed dramatically in the past decade. Major advances in research about human cognition and intelligence have helped cognitive psychologists develop a model of learning that views children, not as the mere receptors of knowledge and information, but also as meaning makers actively engaged in constructing their own learning (Resnick, 1987).

Teachers who use this model of learning believe that prior experience is the template against which much new learning is developed. As a result, they make special efforts to get to know their students well and to learn to see the world as the students see it. Keeping their perspective as adults, they also take on the perspective of students and work to make the connections explicit between the two world views.

Advances in understanding the physiology of the brain and the complexity of intelligence have also contributed to the knowledge base of teaching by bringing new importance to designing environments that help students become "smart." While teaching will never lose its intuitive and speculative dimensions, it now has a developing research base that gives teachers more tools for work and earns more credibility for teaching as a profession. Teaching remains messy, complex, and recursive work. It is still more art than science. Nevertheless, the transitions that teachers are making (see Figure 2.1) hold great promise for rethinking and clarifying what it means to be a teacher.

NEW REALITIES, NEW CHALLENGES

Change is always accompanied by challenge. As teachers begin to chart a new course, they often find themselves confronting old habits,

---

FIGURE 2.1

THE NEW SOCIAL REALITIES OF TEACHING

From	To
Individualism	Professional community
Teaching at the center	Learning at the center
Technical work	Inquiry into practice
Controlled work	Accountability
Managed work	Leadership
Classroom concerns	Whole-school concerns and beyond
A weak knowledge base	A broad knowledge base

---

attitudes, and behaviors in themselves and in each other. They struggle as they abandon old rules and rituals and invent new ones to match their evolving ideas about teaching and learning. They face the challenges that come with learning new ways of thinking and acting, alone and together. Below we discuss some of the challenges teachers face every day, quoting extensively from Lynne Miller's 1994 interviews and conversations with teachers.

Dealing With Conflict

Conflict is inevitable in any major change effort. In schools where practice and belief become topics for public conversation, teachers often find out things out about their colleagues and themselves that they had never suspected.

> I've worked next to John for 20 years, and I never knew he held such views about teaching math. I just assumed that since we got along so well that we agreed about what to teach and how to teach it. When we sat down as a department to decide on student outcomes, all hell broke loose. Here we were, a group of compatible English teachers, unable to agree about the importance of a comma—let alone what to read in 11th grade. We all used the phrase "Every student can learn" and nodded in agreement as one of us said it out loud. Then we tried to figure out what to do with kids who couldn't read at the end of 1st grade, and it became obvious that we had different ideas about things as basic as the words *every* and *learn*.

This level of conflict often surprises staff that have been congenial in the past. But congeniality and collegiality are not the same thing. As professional colleagues, teachers have to discuss their beliefs out loud and reach agreement about the direction of the whole school. Teachers are not, as a rule, prepared to do this. In fact, they often become masters at denying conflict and dismissing any disagreement as a "communications problem." Conflict has usually been viewed as a morale killer and something to be avoided or immediately resolved. In schools that are reforming, teachers learn how to manage conflict, not how to resolve it. They try to use conflict productively and to accept it as part of the dailiness of life in school. While this may seem difficult, it is a necessary skill that, with practice and commitment, can be learned.

Thinking Systematically

Teachers in schools that are restructuring also learn that all of school life is connected. Curriculum and instruction, staff development, school structure and governance, scheduling and bus schedules, subject areas and grade levels, teachers and students, school and community—all affect each other. It is not possible to change one thing at a time without affecting the whole school. One high school teacher explains:

> We decided to change from 45-minute periods to 90-minute periods. Other schools in the area had done so, and the teachers said they preferred having long periods of instructional time. So, we made the change in September. By October, most of us were miserable. We had no idea what to do with all that time. The schedule didn't allow for lab time in science, so we had to eliminate our AP biology class. Lunch became interminable; kids had too much time on their hands; discipline suddenly became an issue when it had not been a problem previously. All of our staff development time was spent complaining about the schedule. We just didn't think through the repercussions of this one simple change.

An elementary principal provides another example.

> We eliminated our early kindergarten program because we felt it was not really developmentally appropriate. We thought that we could equalize the size of the four kindergarten classes and deliver a better program. We didn't count on the district filling each class to capacity. And we didn't bargain for the problems that having "early K" kids in our classes would entail. We had become used to having "ready" students. We didn't have a clue about how to deal

with the "unready." We didn't have the resources needed to serve these kids well. We had to rethink our curriculum on the spot, make adjustments we weren't prepared for, and think about the repercussions of this one step for the entire school, K–5. What does this mean for first grade? Second? Do we look at retention as an option, even though we rejected it last year?

Teachers are learning that one change, whether it focuses on the whole school or on one grade level, never remains only one change. It is transformed into many changes taking place at the same time. Group planning involves people in thinking strategically, in making connections, and in predicting unintended results of intended changes. This kind of thinking is not intuitive—especially for people who have been thinking in terms of *my* classroom and *my* kids for most of their professional lives. Thinking systemically needs to be learned.

Including Everyone

There are always some teachers in a building who are more eager than others to try something new, to take risks, and to challenge their own traditions as teachers. And there are always some teachers who are more cautious, who want more data, and who are less certain that new is better. Because it is so difficult for these two different groups of people to agree on the pace of change, there is a tendency to do "pilot" programs that do not involve the whole school and make no provisions for doing so. Too often, these pilots remain outside the mainstream, threatening people in the rest of the school and causing resentment. Eventually most of these programs collapse, not from lack of value but from lack of support. New behaviors are difficult to acquire, and in the end it is easier to return to old habits than to embrace new ones.

> We started a school-within-a-school to accelerate change. Those of us involved in the project were excited about it and committed enormous energy and time to the program. We managed to get a lighter teaching load so we could do the job well. We also convinced the powers that be to let us use an alternative bell schedule and grading system. Things were fine when we were planning, but once our program actually started there was resentment and sabotage. We lasted two tumultuous years. The resource room teacher and I decided to include the special ed. kids and my kids in one classroom. The principal gave her okay. We had just gotten

started when the district special ed. director got upset because she wasn't involved. Then the fourth grade teachers got upset because they thought this meant they would have to do what I did the next year. We continued the program for a year but decided there was too much bad feeling to do it again this year.

Teachers are coming to recognize that it is better to include everyone in planning and run the risk of slowing things down than it is to move ahead with a small group and run the risk of failing. In some schools, faculties have developed a consensus model of decision making in which all teachers agree publicly to allow a small group to move ahead and not to undermine the effort. This kind of mechanism frees up leading-edge reformers to try something new without alienating their colleagues. It is a way to promote community and entrepreneurship at the same time.

Using and Sharing Ideas

Ideas propel change. Teachers in schools that are reforming are often inspired by the ideas of people from outside their school. Ted Sizer's maxim (1984) "Less is more" has stimulated a rethinking of what we teach and how we teach it. Joseph McDonald's "planning backwards" model (1991) has given teachers a concrete method for designing learning for students. Notions such as authentic assessments, outcomes-based education, standards and benchmarks, habits of mind, and portfolios and exhibitions have all influenced teacher practice in substantial ways. This openness to ideas from outside is an important characteristic of teachers who are in the process of change.

But ideas are generated from inside the school as well as from outside. Notions within a faculty about learning, assessment, and instruction can also provide the stimulus for action. In fact, in many schools, teachers begin with ideas from outside and then modify them to meet their own needs. There is a healthy tension that emerges between knowledge developed from within the school and knowledge that comes from the outside.

The theoreticians clarify theory; they don't clarify practice. We're in the middle of solving an important problem. We began by listening to outside experts. They had some good ideas. But, quite, truthfully, the further I get into this, the clearer it becomes that they have nothing to tell me now. We all have to do the work ourselves now. We're the experts about practice.

Teachers, like the one quoted above, are often disturbed about the limitations of good ideas, and they express concern about the disconnection between what external experts espouse and what internal practitioners experience. As they live through the complexity of figuring out how to implement powerful ideas, they confront the tension between theory and practice. In the best of circumstances, they learn how practice informs theory and how theory informs practice. They develop an appreciation of the knowledge that outsiders can provide. In other situations, teachers grow suspicious of outside experts and rely more on their own insights. But all teachers in schools that are reforming learn to decide what ideas are most useful, when to adopt them, and when to modify them.

Working Bottom-Up and Top-Down

Teachers in schools that are transforming are learning that grass-roots efforts must be combined with administrative initiatives. Bottom-up changes may work for a while, but they often get blocked in the structural bureaucracy that surrounds most schools. Top-down strategies may garner a great deal of publicity and early support, but they are easily undermined by disapproving teachers. Many educators are drawn to the movement to change schools because they see in it the promise of democratic decision making. They quickly learn, however, that good ideas and intentions are not enough. It is important to have enabling policies as well (Darling-Hammond & McLaughlin, 1995).

> Our superintendent provided the time and the opportunity for us to talk together about kids and learning. When we proposed changes in the high school day, she advocated for us with the school board. When we needed extra time to talk and plan together, she promoted a new staff development plan. She brought in outside people for targeted seminars. She supported our new report card, our initial parent interviews. She even managed to change the school calendar. It's hard to tell what started with her and what started with us. She kept the tigers at bay, although most of the time she didn't even tell us they were there. We had been working with developing student outcomes for some time. When our superintendent suggested we have community forums to develop life-role outcomes, I thought at first that she was stealing our thunder. I realize now that this was a very smart strategy for preparing the community for what we wanted to do. While some of the life-role outcomes don't gel with ours, they provide a necessary framework for what we want to do. Now I can connect everything we're

---

FIGURE 2.2

NEW CHALLENGES FOR THE NEW SOCIAL REALITIES
OF TEACHING

- ◆ Dealing with conflict
- ◆ Thinking systematically
- ◆ Including everyone
- ◆ Using and sharing ideas
- ◆ Working bottom-up and top-down
- ◆ Keeping perspective amid the confusion

---

doing in class with what the community said it wanted. The super-intendent followed our lead and worked the system for us. We never had to fight the way other schools and districts have.

By trial and error, teachers and administrators are developing ways of working together and supporting each other. They are learning that people have to work at the top and at the bottom to make things happen. This means that old adversarial patterns need to be broken and that new norms of behavior have to be honored.

Keeping Perspective Amid the Confusion

Teachers in schools that are restructuring are working together to maintain a healthy perspective on their work and their struggle. They are learning to listen to one another and to solve problems together. And they are finding that the best way to keep a good perspective is to focus on the work their students produce. At a 1993 gathering in Gorham, Maine, of teachers who are engaged in changing their schools around student work and learning (see Figure 2.2), Rick Lear, an observer from the Coalition of Essential Schools, offered these three rules-of-thumb:

It'll be harder than you think.
You'll wish you never started.
You'll realize you couldn't not do it.

VIEWS FROM PRACTICE

In this section we present the stories of two teachers who are moving from one set of social realities to another and from one set of challenges to another. The teachers are from different parts of the country and from different kinds of schools. Sally Carruthers teaches second grade on the West Coast; her story is based on Ann Lieberman's 1998 field notes and interviews. Rich Bishop teaches high school science on the East Coast; his story is based on Lynne Miller's 1993–1994 field notes and interviews. Both teachers are struggling with issues of accountability, learning, leadership, and inquiry within schools that are, themselves, making transitions. Sally used a district mandate to expand her own practice. She became frustrated as she struggled to change, discovering in the process that she needed a level of support that neither she nor the district anticipated. Rich is in a very different situation. Having initiated change from within and being the beneficiary of strong district support, he discovered that as old problems are solved, new ones are created. The new problems often require a more fundamental rethinking of schools and classrooms than even he had anticipated. These teachers' stories show that whether change is top-down or bottom-up, it is always filled with uncertainty. As teachers learn new ways of doing business, they are learning how to be teachers all over again.

Sally Carruthers

Sally Carruthers teaches at Hillside Elementary School in the suburb of a city in California. Having come to the school 10 years ago when she was 23 years old, Sally is now the most experienced staff member in a staff that has many new young teachers. Her entire career as a teacher has been at Hillside. She has seen several principals come and go. She worked well with the last principal, and she has a good relationship with the new one, who is still learning the ropes. Although Sally has developed a sophistication about the culture of her school and district, she has her head and heart firmly in her classroom.

Three years ago, the district embarked on an ambitious project to refocus how early literacy was taught and assessed. Sally and her colleagues were uncertain about the new methods being promoted or why they were deemed necessary.

> I think the whole idea of Whole Language was being challenged, but I don't know the specifics. Maybe it was also that students had to be at grade level. But I am not really sure. We didn't have any assessments district wide.

Sally was one of several teachers chosen from different schools to attend four training days at the district office. They were to learn about the latest strategies in teaching literacy.

> At those training days we were introduced to ideas such as guided reading, running record, shared reading, phonemic awareness, and a whole assessment package which was to provide data for better diagnosis of students' learning problems and consequent better teaching. They threw out 10–15 new concepts. We had an hour on the running record, an hour on directed reading.... There was vocabulary that none of us had ever heard. Training was over and we were supposed to go back to our classrooms and do it. Needless to say, we all felt overwhelmed and anxious. I am lucky. I have a lot of friends who are teachers. One of them said to me, "Just pick one idea, and—after you really understand it and know how to use it in the classroom—pick another. It will take 10 years."

Sally thought that this was helpful advice, but she was still troubled by the lack of follow-up or classroom support for implementing any of the ideas from her four-day training. On her own, she decided to learn how to use the running record.

> I knew I was fumbling, but it was clearly the most valuable tool I had been exposed to in the last 10 years. It allows you to get very specific information on what a child is using to decode and find meaning. You look at each error a child makes when they read, and you then can differentiate from errors of structure, meaning, visual or syntactical errors. It can really guide your instructions. It is a lot more time-consuming, but it is much more focused.

For Sally, learning something new came as a mixed blessing. Although she had become a more proficient diagnostician of reading problems, she felt pangs of uncertainty. No one had ever been in her class to watch her do a running record. She wondered, "Am I making this all up?" She appreciated having a tool that pinpointed the types of errors students were making on their way to becoming proficient readers, and she liked having specific data to report to parents. But, she thought, "I still need help. I am basically on my own."

Now in the third year of the reform effort on early literacy, many of Sally's colleagues feel overwhelmed and frustrated. Sally, however, has begun to use the running record with enough success to see its benefits. To reinforce the literacy initiative, she has been selected to be a Lead Teacher on literacy for her school. Lead Teachers are responsible for collecting assessments twice a year from each teacher at their school. These assessments are used by the district to provide data on all students' literacy scores, and they are expected to be used by teachers as tools for reporting to parents as well as for organizing instruction based on diagnosed needs. Currently, Lead Teachers have been offered support for 7 days of training on how to become a "cognitive coach." The district believes that Lead Teachers should learn the skills and abilities of coaching. Sally, having just learned how to use the running record, wonders how all this training will help and whether she wants to assume a role beyond her classroom.

> Do I want this? When am I supposed to coach anyone? I need someone to come in and coach me. I love to plan, but none of us have time. I am fortunate. We have a group of teachers who really trust each other, but we meet infrequently. We don't implement these ideas because we don't have time. Every year there is a different focus.

Sally is dealing with many issues at once. As a cognitive coach, she is expected to organize a way to help other teachers in her school. Inherent in the coaching model is the ability to coach other teachers on a variety of teaching, learning, and other school problems. But the examples given in the training Sally received are only about lessons, while the other teachers in her school are struggling with personal as well as instructional questions. Sally needs to find the time to coach, and she worries that she is not qualified.

> Just because we hear ideas, there is a big assumption that we understand them. And then there is a further assumption that we can just go back to our school and do it. The district really believes in modeling and supporting teachers, yet, you need to see a demonstration, try it out, reflect on it, try it again, talk to someone, assess its utility. What we need is to hear something in the morning and try it out in the afternoon. When we get back to our classroom, we have to deal with our own problems.

In the midst of Sally's struggle to do well with her own 20 children in her class (12 boys and 8 girls), she is now being groomed to "lead" her colleagues. She asks:

What do people want? They do want their role clarified and defined. If we are to lead we need more time to practice how to work with others. We had great cognitive training, but we have no time to use it. We are changing our teaching practices and how we relate to each other at the same time. It is a lot of unknown and has taken a lot of time. It sounds good, it looks good—but does it really reach classroom practice enough to make a difference in our work with students?

Rich Bishop

Rich Bishop teaches at Seaside High School in a mixed coastal community in New England. Like many other schools, Seaside has earned a reputation for academic excellence because of its top graduates who go on to select colleges and universities. About 4 years ago, the high school faculty set a course for itself that challenged many of its long-held beliefs and practices.

> We began by looking at restructuring as an idea. Is there a better way to do things than we do now? Someone brought in the Copernican Plan. I was intrigued. No one actually wanted to do this, but we were willing to play with ideas. That was the "moment of creativity." A loosely formed group was started— a loose-knit group to look at what we were doing and can we do it better.

This was the first time a group of faculty had convened across the subject areas in order to consider an educational issue affecting the whole school. The group met for almost a year, and most of its activity consisted of sitting around a table and talking together about what they did and did not know. They were taken with big ideas and gave themselves time to examine them closely.

> We were intrigued by Grant Wiggins, William Spady, Howard Gardner, and others who have ideas about how kids learn. There was no pressure for us to get anything done by next week. We gave each other permission to admit that we didn't know much and that nobody knows how to do this—put these ideas into practice. If there were any rules, it was these: go at your own pace, think locally, admit ignorance.

After months of talking and reading together, the group agreed on assessment as a starting point for its work.

> We talked about assessment. Kids know something and it's our business to find out what they know and start from there. From that entry point, our debate focused on content and process. Is content important? What content is important? Process matters, but you can't demonstrate nothing. In many ways it was a false debate, but it sure got us going deeper with each other about things that matter.

Rich and his colleague Will took it upon themselves to put these ideas about assessment into action. They decided to replace the traditional 9th- and 10th-grade sequence of courses with a science literacy program based on the concept of "planning backwards." They envisioned a common 2-year learning experience designed for all students that would lead to differentiated course selection in the 11th and 12th grades. The new program was to be co-taught and co-planned. Rich and Will began by attending to the development of outcomes for scientific literacy.

> We looked at the outcomes being developed by AAAS [American Association for the Advancement of Science] and NSTA [National Science Teachers Association]. We tweaked them and changed them. We established a community advisory board of scientists and engineers to help us. We ultimately—and this was after a lot of trial and error—came up with six outcomes for scientific literacy. It was only after we did all of this that we realized that developing outcomes was the easy part. You can put them in a file cabinet next to all those scope and sequence charts we used to work so hard on and never see or use them again. That's when we realized that we had to head for assessments and standards.

As they headed for assessment, Rick and Will faced two immediate problems: how to define scientific literacy and how to guarantee it for all students. Other questions followed: If they believe in assessments being connected to real life, what do these assessments look like? How are they different from the trusted measures they had been using? How are the assessments to be used? As summative measures? As formative devices? How are grades to be determined for the transcript and official record?

We finally have answered to our satisfaction, What does it mean to be scientifically literate? We not only have six outcomes, but we also have six assessments and standards of quality work for each. We structure our classroom around the assessments. Students acquire the knowledge and skills they need to complete the assessments and have time to practice along the way. We are pretty confident that if kids complete the assessments to the standard of quality we've defined, they leave the program as scientifically literate. We even have figured a way around the report card. We give an alternative report card for each of the grading periods. It's not till the final report card that we enter a letter grade. It's not perfect, but it's getting there. It's like living in a country with two currencies.

Having resolved one set of dilemmas, Rick and Will had little time to rejoice. Almost immediately, they confronted new challenges.

What hit us this year, square in the face, were extremely challenging freshmen. Very quickly, we came to the conclusion that we didn't know the way to get some of this population through the six outcomes within 2 years. In the old days, we'd have a special class for them and if they came regularly and didn't kill anyone, we'd give them a D. But now, we say to ourselves, "Do we really believe that all kids can learn?" "Do we think all can be 'scientifically literate'?" If we give them a D, then we'll be graduating students who aren't literate.

It became a moral dilemma. I felt myself sliding with the kids. I'd watch them and almost say, "If you'll just do this, then I'll pass you." But I didn't say that. Instead I said, "Make no mistake about it. This is what you have to do." I showed them the product. "If you don't do this level of work, you will not graduate. I believe you can do it. I believe we can all do it 'together.' I'll be teaching here another 20 years, at least. I have all the time in the world for you to achieve success. How much time do you have?" It was a profound encounter. For many, it was the first time they were told what they had to do. It was important for the kids to hear the message, but more important for the staff to make that decision.

Rich and Will are still struggling with how best to deal with their freshman. They realize that the structure of the school needs to change more dramatically than it has in order to accommodate these students and their learning needs. Right now, they are trapped in an old structure as they try to create a new one. Rich's metaphor of a country working with dual currencies extends beyond report card grades; it captures the atmosphere of the whole school in the midst of change. For the first time, Rich finds himself in conflict with many of his colleagues who do not want to move so quickly and are not ready to make so radical a transformation.

The focus on assessment has had a powerful impact on how Rich teaches and thinks about teaching. The major difference has to do with a sense of purpose.

> If you come to my class on a given day, it might not look all that different from other science classes. You might see me showing kids how to write a lab report or how to use a Bunsen burner. The difference is that everything that happens is tied to a purpose; it's connected to an assessment; it's to prepare for a life role.

For example, one of the outcomes of the science program is to apply science process and manipulation skills. The exit assessment asks the students to work as members of a research team and write a lab report that identifies procedures used to identify eight unknown substances for the director of the lab. To prepare for the assessments, students must learn to work collaboratively, become familiar with lab procedures and instruments, acquire skills as technical writers, and master basic knowledge about the attributes of chemical substances. On any given day, then, the students may be doing what appears to be "traditional" schoolwork, but they are doing it for different ends.

> It's all up front. They know that come November, they have to identify eight unknown substances. This is what you're gonna have to know and be able to do. You'll have to work in groups. This is what cooperation and collaboration look like. It's practice for "the big game." There are no surprises. Everything has a purpose and we all know what it is—teachers and students and parents.

Rich's work in the scientific literacy program has extended to his other classes as well. His class in advanced physics, when judged by its content and intensity, is a traditional course for high-achieving science students. Yet, the norms of assessment and teaching are by no means traditional. Expectations are made public, assessments are given before instruction begins, and students are placed in charge of learning. Rich's job is to make learning accessible. For instance, instead of requiring a physics notebook, Rich lets students know that they are responsible for organizing their knowledge.

> I have kids who put together wonderful notebooks, and they tell me that they never took this seriously before. Because they know what they have to know in advance, they can plan for knowing it. One student who used to get D's on his notebooks wrote in his reflections to me, "Knowing I can use my notes during a test has improved my study habits because I try to reorganize my notes— something I never did before. So they flow and make sense to me." I have other kids who don't need a notebook. They get it all from hearing it the first time. So, I've let go of the sacred cow of the physics notebook. I no longer make it a requirement. What is required is that students develop tools that help them and that they use them to complete assessments.

Rich also encourages students to use a wide range of materials and resources to solve problems in physics. He views his class as a physics lab and his students as practicing scientists.

> When a teacher gives a test, what's the first thing he says? "Clear your desk!" Now when an engineer has to design a bridge, does he clear his desk? No! He covers his desk with sources of information and tools that will assist him. That's how I run my class— more like real life and less like school. I tell kids not to memorize. If you use something enough, you memorize. When do people sit down and memorize their best friend's phone number?

For Rich, teaching and learning have to do with three important premises: all kids can learn at a high level; time is the variable; and the outcomes and assessment standards are constant. Schools have the power to ensure that all kids are successful at learning. These premises hold true in a traditional physics class as well as in a more experimental program in scientific literacy.

The work that Rich and his colleagues have taken on is not simple or straightforward. They are engaged in a radical reconfiguring of teaching and learning in that hardest to penetrate of institutions:

the successful suburban high school. As his narrative illustrates, challenge begets challenge.

> How I really feel is that I am in the middle of solving a complex problem. It's like solving a problem in physics. It's an engineering problem. We're designing a machine and we have to understand the principles—or maybe we have to readjust the principles. But we have to build the new machine, because the old one just doesn't work anymore.

RECREATING LEADERSHIP
Values, Visions, and Action

◆ ◆ ◆ ◆ ◆

Educational leaders must create artful ways to reweave organizational tapestries from old traditions, current realities, and future vision. This work cannot be done by clinging to old ways, emulating principles from effective schools and excellent companies, or divining futuristic images from what we imagine the next decades will be like. Rather, it takes a collective look backward, inward, and ahead. It is a process of transformation.

Terrence E. Deal, from "Healing Our Schools:
Restoring the Heart" in *Schools as Collaborative Cultures,*
A. Lieberman (Ed.)

IN *Teachers: Their World and Their Work* (Lieberman & Miller, 1984), we stressed the importance of the school principal in the lives of teachers. At that time, the notion of "the principal as instructional leader" had gained prominence as one of the variables that determined school effectiveness (Lezotte et al., 1980; Rutter, Maughan, Mortimer, Ouston, & Smith 1979). We noted, however, that this idea was more myth than reality for most principals and that instructional leadership—if it occurred at all—took place "between the cracks and around the corners of the job." The principals we interviewed knew that what they ought to be doing was not what they were actually doing and that what they were doing was not enough. Most principals knew:

- they ought to be leaders; but more likely they were managers
- they ought to be helpers, supporters, and developers; but more often they were supervisors and evaluators
- they ought to share knowledge; but they tended to keep secrets
- they ought to be democratic; but circumstances sometimes forced them to be autocratic

- they ought to show concern for individual problems and individual growth; but because they were in charge of the whole school, they had to sacrifice personal vision for a more pragmatic view
- they ought to do long-range thinking; but frequently they had to make short-range, even instantaneous, decisions to keep small brush fires from becoming conflagrations
- they ought to be colleagues; but often they were bosses
- they ought to be innovators; but they were maintaining the status quo
- they ought to be champions of ideas: in reality they were masters of the concrete, paying attention to detail before worrying about abstractions

These dichotomies still exist today. Different principals resolve them in different ways. A large number choose to accept the givens of their present world and disparage ideals and visions that challenge that reality. They opt to be good managers and not good leaders: they support and maintain the status quo and resist attempts to change things. They neither initiate nor actively support school improvements. Other principals continue their usual ways of doing business, with one eye cocked toward other possibilities. By so doing, they leave themselves open to outside influences, to taking a step toward assertive leadership, questioning the status quo, and improving and changing schools. While they do not initiate improvement activities, they are often won over by enthusiastic faculty with new ideas, and they lend their support to the programs and plans of others. While the latter type of principal is preferable to the former, neither has the capacity to lead schools towards new realities of schooling and teaching.

What is required is a new kind of leadership, principals who are willing to commit to leading for student accomplishment, for organizational health, for professional learning, and for long-range and deep improvements. These leaders work seriously to support the transformation of schooling and teaching and understand the importance of helping to build a learning community that includes all teachers and students. These are not "lone rangers" who depend on charisma and individual genius to transform schools. Rather, they are collaborative learners and teachers who advocate for democratic principles. They work diligently with their faculty and their community to make bold visions a reality.

TEACHER-DIRECTORS IN "CREATED SCHOOLS"

A powerful example of this kind of leadership has been documented in groups of newly created schools in New York City (Lieberman, Falk, & Alexander, 1994). One of these, Central Park East Elementary School, was founded in 1985 in East Harlem by Debbie Meier. The school was created from scratch to develop a democratic learning community that honors diversity and provides for the whole child. It is based on principles of student and teacher learning and the development and use of assessments to guide instruction. Central Park East inspired a "small schools movement" in New York City that led to the formation of the Center of Collaborative Education (CCE). All member schools are newly created and subscribe to a common core of beliefs and practices similar to those of Central Park East.

An outstanding characteristic of the CCE schools is that they do not have traditional principals.

> Instead they have teacher-directors who are required to simultaneously balance a variety of skills and abilities: administrative skills (overseeing paperwork, buses, schedules), political skills (educating and negotiating with stakeholders in the educational enterprise, both inside and outside of their schools), pedagogical understandings (providing ongoing professional development and support to teachers), and a vision for the future (anticipating and preparing for new developments). (Lieberman, Falk, & Alexander, 1994, p. 12)

The teacher-directors face challenges from inside and outside. They are constantly managing conflict, acknowledging struggle, advocating for children and families, supporting and challenging teachers, and working to maintain a safe, orderly, and smoothly functioning organization in an often unstable environment. They view themselves as stewards of the school. They protect their vision and values in the face of conflicting district policies and commitments.

> They must simultaneously fulfill the requirements for survival in the established system and struggle to develop and maintain an "alternate" community that enacts, takes risks, and works to establish practices that question categorization of students, fragmentation of the school program, and a standardized conception of knowledge and learning. (Lieberman, Falk, & Alexander, 1994, p. 17)

The CCE teacher-directors represent a new kind of leadership for a new kind of school. Although their context is different from that of most public schools, they can teach some important lessons. They demonstrate the power of democratic and visionary leadership; they provide evidence that even in the most turbulent and challenging urban setting, it is possible to educate all children well.

INNOVATIVE PRINCIPALS IN "RECREATED SCHOOLS"

Most teachers and principals work in schools that are not newly created. These schools have long histories and deeply rooted traditions and cultures. They need strong leaders who can help build learning communities and help lead efforts to *recreate* schooling. Our work with schools that are reforming has introduced us to many such leaders. They have the same qualities of leadership as the CCE teacher-directors. Where they differ is in how they enter a school and take the lead in its transformation. Many of the principals we interviewed spoke of having an "entry plan," a strategic approach to data collection that enabled them to learn the culture of the school before they tried to effect change. Below, we profile three principals and describe how they chose to enter their schools as new principals with an agenda for change (Miller, field notes, 1992–95).

Joy Roemer's entry set the stage for a 10-year transformation process in a disadvantaged regional high school. When she arrived at the school, she was shocked by the consistently low aspirations of both students and staff. She decided to spend her first year listening to the community. What she heard were expressions of anger and disappointment. Joy remembers:

> They felt the school had failed them in the past and was now failing their children. This intergenerational distress was almost visceral. People were disenfranchised; they lacked trust; they felt a history of broken promises and dashed hopes. Few of the teachers lived in the community; most commuted from middle-class neighborhoods. I even heard one teacher refer to the schools as "McDonald's High School," because that's where the students were headed after graduation.

By working *from* the community *into* the school, Joy gathered support for the reforms she advocated. She realized that the best way to leverage change was through the community. The vision and practices she proposed received widespread support. Now, 10 years later, a significant majority of the students attend post-secondary schools; all have plans for their lives after graduation; state assessment scores have risen; the school has acquired a new reputation in the region. But such progress did not come without cost. Some teachers were upset over the changes and transferred to other schools in the district. They were quickly replaced by teachers from outside the system and by others from within the district who agreed with the new direction of the school. Joy now had a fully committed faculty, ensuring that the values and practices she had espoused would endure.

Linda Mutter inherited a middle-school principalship when the previous principal left under public duress. A highly successful elementary principal in the district, she was "volunteered" into the vacant position by the superintendent. Linda was eager to meet the challenge and took the job. Long viewed as the weak link in the district, the school was struggling with many of the issues endemic to middle-level education: content versus process, teams versus departments, academic rigor versus emotional support, interdisciplinary work versus traditional subject-matter distinctions. The school needed a strong leader. Linda began by visiting each classroom in her building. She recounts:

> By seeing people teach, I could figure out who my natural allies were. If I found a teacher who genuinely liked kids, who had a passion for what she was teaching, and who could help kids make connections, I knew I had an ally. The next year when I began to form committees to guide restructuring, I was able to place these allies in leadership positions. Many of them had never assumed leadership before. They were just good teachers; they were exactly the people I needed to help lead change.

Now in her fifth year, Linda and her allies have guided the school toward changes in teaming, teaching, curriculum planning, assessment practices, and student-grouping policies. Perhaps the most ambitious plan, now being realized, is to have every teacher take responsibility for literacy instruction. To reach this goal, the entire staff learned how to teach literacy. Besides training in new skills, this required a reconceptualization of teaching roles. Linda's point of entry allowed her to identify allies among the faculty who helped her lead the reform process.

David Sewell became a principal after 15 years as an accomplished teacher. He applied for the position on a whim, having had no previous administrative experience. Now in his sixth year as principal, he leads a K–6 school in a predominantly working-class area, adjacent to a large city. David's entry plan had him meeting with each teacher during the summer preceding his first academic year at the school. Listening to the teachers, David discovered that they had been infantilized by the previous principal, although they were all fond of him. When they were asked to name a change they would like to see in the school, none could think beyond unlocking the supply cabinet and having access to the copying machine. David decided to start where the teachers were and not where he wanted them to be. He announced at the first faculty meeting that both the supply closet and the copying machine would be operated on the honor system, with unmediated access for all staff.

With small steps like these David began to forge a new culture in the school based on respect and trust. He paid close attention to what the faculty said, and in response the faculty paid attention to him. In the next few years, there was virtually no staff turnover; yet the school changed significantly. The staff began to work together on small projects and on larger ones. Grade-level teams were strengthened; staff meetings focused on student work; teachers worked continuously on the curriculum and designed and used common assessments. David's point of entry allowed him to listen to the teachers and, by respecting them and treating them as colleagues, to build on their strengths.

Joy, Linda, and David are all engaged in the task of helping to recreate their schools. They chose different ways to begin: through the community, by identifying allies, and by listening closely to teachers. All were successful, demonstrating that there is no one ideal entry point for initiating change and there is no one best way to lead a school.

LEADING FROM VALUES AND VISIONS

The school leaders we have studied and worked with, in both "created" and "recreated" schools, all hold strong beliefs about children and the democratic mission of schools. They are all clear in their expectation that schools should educate everyone to high standards. They believe that all children have the capacity to learn and that schools have the obligation to teach students well, despite conditions beyond their control. They support full inclusion, heterogeneous grouping, and full access to a "thinking curriculum." They reject the notions that excellence should be rationed, that educational triage is acceptable, that labeling and sorting children is part of the regularity of schooling, and that schools cannot undo the damage of difficult life circumstances. They recognize and honor differences but do not use difference as an excuse for reduced expectations and aspirations. A CCE teacher-director expresses values this way:

> We have based our theories about school on what we think to be true about human learning. Certain kinds of school environments speak to what's true about human learning and help it emerge so that in the process of teaching children, and thinking about teaching children, and thinking about themselves as learners, teachers connect to who they are as learners. (Lieberman, Falk, & Alexander, 1994, p. 11)

At CCE Schools, the teacher-directors enact their beliefs daily through their interactions with teachers, students, and parents. They provide time for the Descriptive Review Process, which involves collaborative discussion and review of individual student issues, concerns, and problems. They promote the development of new standards for assessments, based on samples of student work. They involve family members through newsletters, conferences, telephone calls, and narrative progress reports. And, most important, like the teacher quoted below, they uphold the vision and values of the school when these are being contested or challenged.

> A parent objected to heterogeneous grouping out of a belief that it didn't best serve her child. She wanted the school to reconsider the practice for the community as a whole. I had to find a way to help her understand that some values are inviolable and form the basis of our school. (Lieberman, Falk, & Alexander, 1994, p. 15)

So, too, principals who are taking the lead in recreating their schools regularly enact their values and visions. They struggle with how to support and respect teachers, giving credence to their opinions, and at the same time challenge and cajole them. For example, Joan Gordon, a high school principal, believes strongly that tracking limits student potential and is a damaging practice. The faculty she leads is open to many forms of restructuring. They have changed the bell schedule, lengthened class periods, and developed shared assessments. But they remain convinced that ability grouping is beneficial to students because it allows them "to learn at their own pace." Joan wanted to honor her faculty's views, but she also wanted to eliminate what she considered a bad practice. She began a program of information and persuasion that included reading and discussion groups, professional development opportunities, and visits to high schools that had given up tracking. None of this had any effect.

Finally, she involved the department heads in an analysis of class enrollments. The data they collected showed that the classes were already more heterogeneous than they had imagined, that several students with above-grade-level scores on standardized tests were in low-ability classes. This discovery led the department chairs to recommend a reduction in the number of levels—from five to three. While recognizing this proposal was a compromise and an intermediate step, Joan supported it and continued to plan for the day when the levels would be reduced further.

Joan and the CCE teacher-directors represent the kind of "cultural leadership" Sergiovanni (1987) describes.

> When observing highly successful school leaders at work, we see that they know the difference between sensible toughness, real toughness, and merely looking tough and acting tough. Real toughness doesn't come from flexing one's muscles simply because one happens to have more power than another. Real toughness is always principled. (pp. 123–124)

CONNECTING LEADING, LEARNING, AND TEACHING

Principals and teachers in schools that are in the midst of change are finding that as they do their work, they are blurring boundaries and forging new connections between leading, learning, and teaching. Their schools are leadership dense organizations. The direction of leadership is the same in these schools as it is in the newly created schools. At the CCE schools, the traditional title of principal has been replaced; the teacher-director is viewed as someone who is rooted in the classroom and who represents the teacher perspective in the management of the school. In schools that are being recreated, though the title of principal remains, the foundations and substance of leadership are being transformed.

Joy Roemer, the high school principal who began her work by winning the support of the community, represents this kind of transformation. She could not have succeeded in changing the structure and practices of her school without the support and leadership of a strong cadre of teachers who shared her commitments. Together, Joy and this stalwart band of teacher-leaders initiated and implemented a new school schedule, revised graduation requirements, introduced new curricula and assessments, and instituted a graduation plan for each student. Teacher leadership became so embedded in the school that when Joy resigned her post, she was succeeded by a team of three teachers who assumed a joint principalship.

Linda Mutter also promoted teacher leadership in her middle school. Equating good teaching with the potential for good leadership, Linda identified and nurtured a group of teachers who later led the restructuring efforts in the school. These teachers are now influencing the district in its reform agenda by serving as conveners of curriculum groups and facilitators of professional development activities. They use their experience at the middle school as the basis for district-wide action. Working at a slower pace, David Sewell and Joan Gordon are also cultivating a culture of teacher leadership. By listening to the staff, they send a message that teacher concerns matter and that teacher knowledge and experience count. David and Joan know that without teacher support and leadership, efforts to change the school will remain at a surface level and go no deeper. Starting with trust and respect, they are building the foundations for new forms of leadership in their schools.

In addition to the roles of leader and teacher, adults in "created" and "recreated" schools have the equally important role of learner. A CCE teacher-director sees the connection this way:

> What we model for kids, I try to model for adults. Good kindergarten practice is also good leadership practice. It's about acknowledging that each has different gifts, strengths, and concerns, and then finding a way to utilize them. It's about giving teachers a sense of understanding, empathy, partnership, belonging. My personal understanding of learner-centered teaching has become my model of leadership. (Lieberman, Falk, & Alexander, 1994, p. 13)

Principals in these schools are attentive to the learning needs of both children and adults. They work to provide a wide variety of arenas for growth and development for themselves and their teachers. They acknowledge the iterative nature of teaching, leading, and learning. The principal of one of the schools we profile in Chapter 1, in a 1995 interview with Lynne Miller, put it this way:

> Our school considers itself a "center of inquiry." What we promote for children in the classroom, we also promote for ourselves. Children inquire about what they see and hear around them and explore what they want to know more about. Adults in our school also inquire and explore. We inquire about how children learn and we explore better ways to help them. My role of principal is to ensure that every teacher has the opportunity to learn, just as every teacher makes that assurance for students. I can lead in that learning, but so can others. And they do.

A VIEW FROM PRACTICE

There is no better way to understand how leadership is being transformed than to look at real-life examples. Here we present an extended view from practice as we follow one principal, Jane Deaken, through a full day at an urban elementary school.

Case Study

Walter Russell is a neighborhood elementary school, grades K through 5, located in a low-income area of a small city that borders a large urban center. A Title I school where 75% of the students go to preschool (including Head Start), Russell has 700 students, 40% white, 45% Hispanic, and 15% Asian, African American, and other. The school has 27 teachers, 12 of them bilingual. In addition there are 10 aides and 5 "novice teachers" (full-time student teachers) on the staff. In 1993 the school applied for and received funds from Senate Bill 1274 (1993) as one of 144 schools in the state that were to restructure according to six dimensions: technology, decision making, program evaluation, accountability systems, professional collaboration, and curriculum and student assessment. This state initiative provided funds for 5 years and also involved the school in a network in which the schools learned from one another and developed a shared agenda. Since 1993 Walter Russell has twice been awarded the title Distinguished School and continues to have visitors coming often to see how the school works. The school is a model of effective leadership and its connection to teaching and learning.

Jane Deaken's day as principal begins early. Here we follow her through one Friday in February that happens to be Valentine's Day. (Ann Lieberman observed Jane Deaken all day as she went about her work. All quotes are as they were spoken by Jane, the visitors, and the teachers.)

7:35 a.m.: The two assistants to the principal are in the main office along with several other adults. They are already welcoming people, taking telephone messages, passing out Valentine candies, accepting flowers that are being delivered for one of the teachers, and talking with parents. The school-day hum has started. The office houses three people in an open space that also includes a long counter now loaded with flowers for three teachers. Toward the back of this room is Jane's small office, decorated with Impressionist prints.

In the classrooms, students are making valentines, giving them out, and waiting impatiently for their class parties. Candy is legitimate in school today, and the expectation is that some of it will be eaten as part of the day's activities. In addition, the lower-grade teachers have created a special day because it is the 100th day of school. There are signs all over the school announcing the accomplishments of these 100 days, and students have made headpieces and paper glasses that spell 100 as well as other assorted decorations. There is a lively buzz throughout the school. One child's parents have arranged a program of song and dance from Brazil for all students that will take place in the multipurpose room. A principal from another school and her whole staff are coming for a visit to learn from Russell. At the same time, the faculty is meeting to prepare for next week's Mid-Year Institute. There they will meet as a school and with the whole district to discuss data, assessments, and student work. To capture time to hold the Institute, the school "banked" time accrued by adding 20 minutes to each school day for students, who will have the week off. This method of banking time has now become institutionalized.

7:40: Jane comes in, moving at a fast pace, with her son, who attends the school. As he goes onto his classroom, the day officially begins. Jane wants to call some parents about their son, Sam, who brought X-men cards to school and sold them to another boy for $20. Jane would like to get the $20 back, return the cards, and let it be known that this is not an activity that should happen at school. Just as she is dialing the number, the principal from the visiting school arrives and is asked to go into the teachers' lounge.

7:50: Jane makes the call to Sam's parents and explains the problem. Fixing this situation is not so simple. Sam's parents think that "a deal is a deal" and are a bit annoyed that there is another view being put forth. Jane intervenes and says, "Would you like to speak with the other parent directly?" She gets the telephone number for the parent. Jane quickly speaks to the school secretary, alerting her that the cards and the money may be returned.

8:00: Two teachers from the visiting school come in to ask where to go. A coordinator who usually works with visitors is ill, so Jane fills the gap. She tells them that the teachers are in grade-level team meetings this morning, working on a protocol process in preparation for the Mid-Level Institute. Jane meets eight other teachers who are visiting and tells them they may have their choice of where they would like to go. She tells them that the school is focused on two big questions: How can we improve our math scores for all children? And, how can we deal with the racial inequities in our school? Jane then asks who would like to meet with the fourth/fifth-grade team and takes three teachers with her to one of the classrooms where the team is meeting.

Jane has been asked by the team to explain what will go on in the Mid-Year Institute when they meet with other fourth- and fifth-grade teachers in the district. This is the first time that Russell faculty will meet to present their work to other district teachers, and they are anxious and excited. They turn to Jane for information and assurance. She explains how the Institute will be organized and quickly reviews the discussion protocols that will be used. She tells them:

> We will have lunch together. Everyone is being asked to bring an assessment. There will be seven to eight people in a group. We will ask of each assessment:
>
> 1. What is this piece of assessment? How is it used?
> 2. What did I learn? About kids? How did I alter my instruction?
>
> If there is any more time, we would ask:
>
> 3. Did you see any trends?
> 4. What similarities did we see?
>
> Someone will be a recorder to write down the highlights.

Jane further reviews the norms they will use: people listen attentively and will have the right to pass if they don't want to speak. She concludes, "We will have break-out groups and share together. I told people to bring something they feel good about." Jane announces three articles they will read—one discusses the use of data and an other, written by a teacher, discusses how she thinks about her math teaching. The third discusses what it means to teach "other people's children." The teachers appear satisfied that they know what to do and are sensitive to the fact that other schools might not be as far advanced as they are. On the way out a teacher comes up to Jane and says she needs to talk with her about Greg. His parents are upset, and she needs to keep Jane informed of what is going on. The student has been behaving violently toward other students. This is a child that they are trying to include in mainstream activities. The school believes strongly in inclusion and has a good track record, so this presents a special problem to solve. Jane invites the teacher to come see her before the day is over.

8:30: Jane walks rapidly back to the teachers' lounge, where the first-grade teachers are meeting in their grade-level team and are also being observed by 10 of the visiting teachers and their principal. Jane describes to the visitors what the team is doing and how they are preparing for next week. She gives them a quick orientation for what they are seeing in the first-grade team and describes the general context of the school.

8:45: Jane makes her way to where the third grade is having its team meeting and gives them the two articles that are to be part of the Mid-Year Institute. Between rooms she meets a teacher who reports suspected child abuse. They talk for a few minutes to plan some follow-up of the case. Both the teacher and Jane express tremendous empathy for the child and puzzle over what they can do.

Jane then goes to attend the meeting with 10 aides and 5 novice teachers who are meeting with a Teacher Leader, who is the Reading Recovery teacher. She wants to explain the Mid-Year Institute to these two groups of people, who, she feels, have an important role to play and who offer different perspectives. She begins with the aides, who represent a broad array of ethnic, racial, and age differences and who all come from the adjoining community.

> Next week we have a Mid-Year Institute. We are preparing a process which we call the protocol. We listen to each other and then we give feedback. Your role is to give honest and direct feedback. Your perspective is extremely important.

She then turns to the novice teachers and reviews for them the central concerns of the school.

> We have set two basic questions for ourselves this year:
>
> 1. We see in all the data we have collected that Anglo kids are doing better than Hispanic and black students. We are asking ourselves: What can we do differently to see that this inequitable pattern changes?
> 2. How can we use math to build on a strength rather than a deficit model?

She explains to both groups that the process they will use is fairly formal. She wants to make certain that they all feel comfortable enough with it to participate and contribute. She explains that on Tuesday parents will be invited to participate and give feedback. For the rest of the week, the work will mostly involve school staffs. On each day, different grade levels will present reports. Wednesday is for K–1; Thursday for 2/3; and Friday for 4/5. Groups will be formed on Tuesday and then continue for the week. The teachers are all familiar with the process, but the aides and novices are not; so Jane takes time to explain step-by-step what will occur.

> Here is exactly what will happen. There will be opportunity for everyone to understand the background of the grade levels and what they are trying to accomplish. People will have time to ask clarifying questions.

She explains that there will be two groups: an inner and an outer circle. The inner circle will present their assessment, while the outer circle listens. This will take 30 minutes. The large outer group will then divide into smaller feedback groups, while the presenting team members walk around and listen in on the feedback discussions. The feedback sessions will be focused on a set of questions posed by the presenting team, and the team will decide what they want to respond to from the feedback they have heard. Jane advises:

> You will be asked to give feedback to the team. You need to give compliments, but also give the "hard" stuff too. The purpose is to make public the tough stuff. Think of a nice way to say the tough stuff. You are a very important group. You can give feedback that is so critical. We need your perspective and how you think about what you hear and what you see. We will have board members, district staff, and researchers from out of town attending the Institute as well.

She encourages the aides to be flexible about when they come in during the Institute, expressing sensitivity to their time commitments and other responsibilities. She ends her discussion of the Institute by giving out the three articles that are to be part of the Mid-Year Institute and prepares them for Lisa Delpit's piece, "The Silenced Dialogue" (1995), which she tells them is difficult but very important. Jane moves on to more immediate concerns, reviews the week's schedule, and then turns to advice about the Internet. The fourth/fifth-grade students have access to the Internet for their work, and she is concerned that everyone understand the rules of use: there will be no pornography and standards of politeness are understood.

9:15: Jane is back in the office talking with the secretary about a sick child in the office. She has called the child's home, but no one is there. They have made arrangements to take care of the child in the small nurse's office.

9:40: Jane prepares for the flag ceremony, which occurs with the whole school in the yard every Friday. She briskly walks to the yard, where all the students and their teachers are gathering. This has become a favorite time to see the whole community together in one place, and a small group of parents has come to watch. Jane goes up to the center of the assemblage:

> Boys and girls, we need everybody's attention. This is a very special day. It is the 100th day of school. The first- and second-grade students have taken a special responsibility on this day and we want to thank them. But first to the pledge. I can't find the flag, so we will pretend it is there.

She leads the pledge of allegiance in English and Spanish. The first graders have prepared a parody of "I've Been Working on the Railroad," and they begin to sing, "We've been working in our classrooms. . . . This is followed by a big drawing to reward students who have done chores around the school. Jane draws from a bowl full of "success tickets." These tickets are given to students for doing a variety of jobs that care for the school. Four students win prizes, and everyone cheers. Jane then announces the Read-a-Thon and encourages students to have fun on their week off and also spend time reading. All students have a chart that encourages them to keep track of reading by providing space to record when they are read to and when they read themselves.

10:00: The younger students go directly to the multi-purpose room for the song and dance presentation. Jane arrives to start the event; the students gather excitedly, seating on the floor and around the tables. In a few hours this room will serve as the cafeteria. Jane speaks:

> This assembly is very special. Today we are going to hear some songs and see dances from a country called Brazil. And tomorrow we are going to have a Love and Unity Festival so don't forget to bring your families to it.

Jane races back to the teachers' lounge to talk with the visitors who have been observing the first-grade team discuss their work on assessments for mathematics. She explains that the school has 700 students in grades K through 5 and describes the racial and ethnic make-up. Then she continues:

> We have been involved as a [Senate Bill] 1274 school. We were to be a demonstration school that showed how to restructure—

to literally reculture a school. What you saw this morning was our attempt to break the isolation of teaching. We know that teaching is a lonely job and an impossible job to do well without having the time and support to constantly improve. It doesn't happen naturally in teaching. One way that helped us was to bank time. We have a late start every Friday, at 9:45, but students come early if their parents work and have no means of day care. During this time they are supervised by nonteaching staff in the playground and art room. In this way, teachers get a chance to get together in the morning and improve their work.

We have grade-level teams that meet twice a month. These teams are led by a Lead Teacher. They receive a stipend. They have a big leadership role. Grade-level teams are run by the teachers. Their agendas are always full. They sometimes elect to have a third meeting after school. Friday morning the school meets as a whole once a month. The aides also have a meeting where they receive information and special training. Every other month there is a cross-grade-level cluster meeting.

There is also a math planning day, once a month. These meetings have helped us become a real community. The grade-level groups are really the backbone of the school. They have helped us change. We also have a voluntary activity called Inquiry Group. This group meets twice a month and is led by a "critical friend," an outside person who asks questions and serves as an informal leader. This group steps back and allows serious reflection on what is going on. It serves as an opportunity for teachers to talk privately about their feelings, their doubts, et cetera. This is being paid for by Annenberg funds. During the time teachers meet here, artists from the community come to teach. In this way there is an enrichment to our school and a value-added set of learnings.

We have been working on literacy for three years. We have set standards for ourselves. We have set our own standards in math and literacy. We have also created an assessment system that matches our standards. Teachers first assessed their own kids in private. We then began to score assessments more publicly. During our Mid-Year Assessment Institute we will look at grade- and school-level trends. We did literacy: now we are doing math. We want to make sure there is real student learning going on.

There are other areas where we work more closely with the community. We have made good strides. We have an active

P.T.A. They do the traditional things. Since 1974 we have had a Bilingual Advisory Council. We are fortunate. We have quality bilingual teachers in every classroom.

At first we offered clubs for the students before school. But it was too much fun. All kids came, and it was too much for us to handle. We had to change it. We had to ask only those parents who didn't have adequate child care in the morning to use the option of coming to school early. The harder part was banking time. Now the whole district is doing it. The dilemma for us is that the district organizes staff development, and we don't go because it is not relevant to where we are.

The visiting principal asks, "How are you bringing in new people?" Jane answers:

We have one asset. We have a partnership with a local university. We have a program where we take their preservice students. We take novices for one year. We buddy mentors and novices and they work with the grade-level teams. In this way we get ample opportunity to see new teachers, and some of them do indeed end up teaching at our school.

When we began we looked at many different frameworks. We looked at national standards, the New Standards Project. We are learning from everyone. We then set our own standards very high. We set a Level 16 for first grade. Every year we make better progress. We designed our own assessment system. We think it helped us see how kids are progressing, and it also helped teaching. We have three assessment points:

1. We keep running records up to Level 24 in third grade.
2. We take writing assessments.
3. We do math assessments.

We score together. This is a great way to trade teaching strategies. We provide progress reports to parents on a 6-point rubric. We try to relate it all together. In the goals and standards, the assessments, Back-to-School night, the same messages are there. Parents need to learn how much support their kids need. Most grading systems are sort and select. When you compare kids against a standard, all students have opportunities to learn; and teachers learn what they need to do to provide a better learning situation for students.

We also have safety nets. We have a Reading Recovery teacher. We provide one-on-one tutoring, if needed. We have teacher aides. We have some high school tutors and volunteers. We have a longer day, a longer year, and summer school. We are a Title I school. But we have upper-middle-class families too. This is most unusual. We have a preschool here and a Head Start too. Seventy-five percent of our students go to preschool. We disaggregate our data by race, ethnicity, gender, and free and reduced lunch.

As an administrator I only go to grade-level teams when I am invited. The school is pretty much teacher-led. I meet with Lead Teachers to get things on the agenda. But it is pretty much their agenda. The grade-level team decides how long the Lead Teachers should be there. Some have been there for 3 years.

11:00: Jane leaves the visiting team and goes to the cafeteria, where the fourth/fifth graders are seeing the Brazilian songs and dances. Two tables of preschoolers are eating lunch at the same time, but they appear to be entertained as they eat. The performers involve the audience; and the students are very responsive to the songs, dances, and instruments that are part of the program.

11:30: Jane meets with a teacher who comes by the office. The teacher is working to integrate an autistic child into her classroom. The school, and this teacher in particular, are adamant about inclusive classrooms. This student is having a difficult time. The teacher thinks he needs a smaller environment with less noise. She is very attentive and very sensitive to his learning needs, but the parents want to work only through their lawyer. Jane listens as they talk about next week's schedule and how to handle this tough situation.

Jane speaks to the nurse, who is taking care of Ben, a child itching from hives. The school has permission to give him Benadryl, but the parent appears not to follow through at home. Jane speaks to a child who has been sent to the office for misbehavior. She says, "This day isn't going too well for you. I will speak with you later." She then goes outside to check on the children who are eating lunch at a table in the schoolyard. Jane notes that the students who bring their lunch eat at tables outside together, while others eat in the cafeteria. She is distressed that this further segregates children.

12:05: Jane returns to her office and finds another student, Wayne, who has been sent there by his teacher. Wayne looks up, and Jane begins, "Wayne, what is going on today?"

"I was playing basketball, and every day Jon keeps hitting me. This time he hit me and I hit him back."

"Have you thought about mediation?"

"That doesn't work for me."

"What will work? Is there something else going on?"

"My mom and I went to the movies and it was sold out. Then we went to the doughnut shop and the place was closed. I hate Jon!"

"Let me do mediation with you and Jon. I think it might work."

Matt and Fred are waiting outside Jane's office. They have been fighting and have been sent to the office. Jane invites them in.

Jane turns to the two of them: "I thought you were friends."

"We were," Matt says. "I have to do everything at home. My mom has a hard time and she is always sick."

Matt has apparently made fun of Fred's parents, who can neither hear nor speak, and the kidding has been answered by making fun of Matt's mother. This has led to the fight.

Jane continues to try to reach conciliation: "Matt, can you agree not to make fun of Fred? And Fred, can you agree that if you have differences, you won't try to settle them by hitting?"

They both nod in agreement. They shake each other's hand, and it is clear that they want to be friends.

"Go tell Trudy [their teacher] about your agreements with each other."

Jane answers a quick telephone call about service learning. And within seconds a woman comes in and explains that a student has taken a nanopet, and the teacher worked it out. Jane goes outside. The schoolyard appears to be a scene of great fun and potential problems. Jane goes up to a group of children. She tells one boy some nice things she has heard about him. He shyly smiles. Jane sees the music teacher and talks to him about a program on Saturday. She then bumps into a girl who is crying. She was hit while playing. Jane suggests that the child wash her face and then go back outside. It is clear it is an accident and that no one is to blame. The incident is handled quickly but sensitively.

12:40: Back in the office a teacher is waiting, standing next to Anthony. She tells Jane that Anthony has taken another child's Valentine candies and eaten them. Anthony has taken other people's things on other occasions too. Jane asks him to stay in the office where she promises to handle the problem.

Five minutes later, Jane is outside again. The physical education teacher mentions that the girl Jane had earlier seen crying did have an accident, on the play equipment. She had her pants pulled down, but not on purpose. That incident is closed with all involved having communicated the same facts. Jane closes the loop. Nothing seems to go unnoticed.

Still outside, Jane walks past some boys playing handball. She points out a boy with special needs who has been totally included in a regular classroom and has been flourishing. She worries that another included child is not making it, and there will be problems. She walks by a few classrooms and sticks her head in to see what the students and teachers are doing. The classrooms are very attractive. It is not just the Valentine's Day parties and decorations that make them so. These are clearly rooms where student work is at the center and on display. Jane enters into a second/third-grade multi-age classroom. In this room, two teachers job share. One teacher works Mondays and Tuesdays; the other works Thursdays and Fridays. They trade every other Wednesday. The father of one of the partners has just died. Jane tells the teacher to tell her partner that whatever timing works for her next week is fine.

Back in the office, Anthony is still there. He is not to go back to his classroom until the party is over. Jane calls the teacher, who says Anthony may come back now. He has been punished by sitting out the party and being sent to the principal's office. Jane has been friendly but firm. As soon as Anthony has gone, Mildred comes in. She is a Title I teacher with outstanding technological skills, who helps compile statistics for Jane and the staff. They discuss what is appropriate to report that would be helpful and meaningful. They decide that there is good news to report. The growth scores that have consistently gone up for whites and for African Americans now show an interesting and important trend. Growth scores have gone up for both groups, but for African Americans they are higher than for whites.

2:32: Jane goes outside for dismissal. Students are getting on buses and being met by parents. There is much casual conversation among teachers, parents, and students. She goes back to her office for a meeting with parents. After the meeting is over, Jane stops by an after-school grade-level meeting and then, with her son in tow, heads home.

PROFESSIONAL DEVELOPMENT FOR THE NEW SOCIAL REALITIES OF TEACHING

◆ ◆ ◆ ◆ ◆

Every individual becomes educated only as he has an opportunity to contribute something from his own experience, no matter how meagre or slender . . . ; and finally that enlightenment comes from the give and take, from the exchange of experience and ideas.

John Dewey, *Democracy and Education*, 1916

NEW FORMS of teaching and leadership take hold when schools honor their adults as learners and provide opportunities for their professional development. As previous chapters show, educators who are engaged in change are under considerable pressure to modify their ideas, actions, and relationships. This does not happen magically; it requires attention and strategic intervention. Conventional in-service is not sufficient to the task. Based on a deficit model, it assumes that teaching is technical work, that development can be packaged, and that teachers are the passive recipients of someone else's knowledge. This approach is clearly inappropriate for transforming teachers. We agree with Judith Warren Little (1993) when she says:

> The well-tested models of skill development, built on the staff development and implementation-of-innovations literature will work reasonably well to introduce those aspects of reform that are "technical" or can be rendered as a repertoire of classroom practices. However, much of what we anticipate in the current reforms does not lend itself to skill training because it is not readily expressed in terms of specific, transferrable skills and practices. (p. 5)

We need another model of professional development, one that is based on the idea of growth-in-practice. Growth-in-practice assumes that teaching is intellectual work and that professional development occurs when teachers have the opportunity to learn from theory and practice as part of their job.

At the present moment in school reform, there is a rush towards results. We do not hesitate to agree that results, especially in student achievement, are at the center of school reform. However, we want to caution against overlooking the importance of process. In our view, if we attend to the underlying processes that support teacher growth and change, we are more likely to accomplish the ends that both teachers and the public want to see for students.

UNDERLYING PROCESSES OF TEACHER DEVELOPMENT

We have identified three underlying processes that help teachers acquire growth-in-practice. Each is described below.

Developing a Professional Community

In Chapter 2, we comment on the need to combine top-down and bottom-up thinking in our efforts to change schools and teaching. Policies from the state, the district, and at the school level can indeed encourage change, but they cannot make it happen; only teachers can. If teachers do not understand the change or think it is reasonable, or if they do not have the time to learn and try out new ideas, the change will not happen. But neither are bottom-up initiatives necessarily enduring. Improvement strategies created in the classroom or at the school level will have a hard time staying alive if they are not eventually supported by policies from above (Darling-Hammond & McLaughlin, 1995). Thus, for change to occur, both policy and practice are necessary, but they must be supported by a viable professional community. McLaughlin and Talbert (1993) found, in a 5-year study of secondary schools, that the development of professional communities of teachers was the essential element that enabled teachers to implement new and more effective ways of working with students. (See Figure 4.1.)

McLaughlin and Talbert (1993) describe how teachers adapt to their students in terms of how they relate to them (authority relations), how they organize their teaching (pedagogy), and how they implement the curriculum. They identify three types of adaptations that teachers make toward their students and their work. The first adaptation describes teachers who enforce traditional standards by giving more rules and

FIGURE 4.1

TEACHERS' RESPONSES TO TODAY'S STUDENTS

Pattern of Adaptation	Domains of Adaptation			Teacher Outcomes
	Relations	Pedagogy	Content	
Enforce traditional standards and tests	Teacher dominates: more rules and sanctions	Transmission teaching: more worksheets and memorization	Emphasis on traditional, fact-based learning	Burnout and cynicism
Lower expectations	Various: relax rules	Various	Watered-down subject matter	Disengagement
Change practices and group norms	Teacher facilitates: construct learning	Active student role: cooperative understanding	Emphasis on conceptual understanding	Efficacy

Note: Reprinted, with permission, from McLaughlin and Talbert, 1993, figure 2.

more punishments as a means of reaching students. Compared with teachers who adapt in other ways, they use more worksheets, memorization, and questions at the end of the chapter. The outcome for these teachers is to suffer burnout and become cynical about teaching.

The second adaptation describes teachers who, in struggling to reach students, decide to lower expectations, each thinking, in effect, "I know the kids can't do it, so I will give them a watered-down version of the curriculum." But because teachers like this have been "developed" by numerous workshops, they know that there are various methods of instruction. So they try them. Mondays and Wednesdays they do cooperative learning and read in jigsaws, but Tuesdays and Thursdays they assign chapters with questions to answer. Friday is test day. These teachers suffer disengagement from their work and often from their students because their mixed strategies leave students confused about how they are to behave and what is expected of them. These teachers are trying to find ways to reach students and, in some ways, exemplify the complexities of how learning for teachers needs to be supported and long term.

The third adaptation describes teachers who decide to rethink content, organization, and the methods of teaching. Teachers like these who actually struggle with how to think about reorganizing their classrooms are involved in the creation of a community (within their department) where teachers relate to one another as colleagues, grow to trust one another, support one another in their attempts to reach the students, try to find new ways of working, and in the process commit themselves to their own continuous learning and development. As teachers develop a professional community among themselves, they discover many new ways to work with students and, in concert with their peers, feel enabled to try things, talk about them, shape them, and gain confidence in changing the way they work with students. These teachers feel far better about their work with students and one another but are continually frustrated, perhaps because there is so much more to do and so little time to do it.

Professional communities develop in a variety of ways. Some begin when teachers decide what standards they believe are important; others when a team of teachers figure out how to group students in a multiage classroom so that time, student activities, and work can be more flexibly arranged; and still others begin when teachers work together on ways to build on each other's skills, abilities, and subject-matter expertise by forming an interdisciplinary unit. A growing body of research has documented the growth of teacher's professional communities in elementary and middle schools and their importance in changing the culture of their schools and the ways teachers work with students (Battistich, Solomon, Kim, Watson, & Schaps, 1995; Little, 1993, 1996; Newmann & Wehlage, 1995). Strong professional communities are built when principals and staff enhance their resources by reinforcing a climate of support and respect for teachers' work and by pursuing a continuous cycle of innovation, feedback, and redesign in curriculum, instruction, and assessment. Teachers' capacity to teach well is enhanced when professional opportunities are *focused, coherent,* and *sustained* (rather than diffused, fragmented and episodic) (Newmann & Wehlage, 1995).

By standing between policies at the top and changed educational practices at the bottom, teachers' professional communities serve as mediators for teachers' interpretations and analyses of student learning. Professional learning is most powerful, long lasting, and sustainable when it occurs as a result of one's being a member of a group of colleagues who struggle together to plan for a given group of students, replacing the traditional isolation of teachers from one another (Lieberman & Miller, 1998; Stokes, Sato, McLaughlin, & Talbert, 1998). These learning communities legitimate "just in time" learning—the kind that is useful on Monday. Peer support that legitimates the struggle and uncertainty accompanying reform helps teachers learn new ways of working with their students.

Combining Inside Knowledge and Outside Knowledge

Teacher growth and development comes about in many ways. Teachers learn from "outside knowledge"—research, reform ideas, conferences, books, workshops, speakers, consultants. But they also learn from "inside knowledge"—by teaching and picking up ideas from fellow teachers and trying them out in their classroom. As Donald Schön (1995) has stated:

> Perhaps there is an epistemology of practice that takes fuller account of the competence practitioners . . . display in situations of uncertainty, complexity, uniqueness, and conflict. Perhaps there is a way of looking at problem-setting and intuitive artistry that presents these activities as describable. (p. 29)

This kind of knowledge has rarely been packaged, but does get passed from teacher to teacher as a part of the lore of teaching. We have yet to build a scholarship of teaching as described and documented by the teachers themselves as some have suggested (Shulman, 1993).

Too much "outside" knowledge feels abstract, too distant and too theoretical, but too much "inside" knowledge can be reduced to merely sharing war stories and situation-specific tales. Both kinds of knowledge are necessary. Asking for outside knowledge is not the same as being told that you *must* learn something. Relying on inside knowledge is not the same as self-absorption; it is a necessary part of creating teachers' sense of community (Ancess, 1998; Cochran-Smith & Lytle, 1993; McLaughlin & Oberman, 1996; Richert, 1991; Shulman, Lotan, & Whitcomb, 1998) and is critical to any sustainable improvements in practice.

Conventional professional development is often solely about learning techniques, as if teaching were a set of technical skills, rather than a complex array of values, knowledge, experience, intuition, and commitment to improve. It is "delivered" in episodic fashion as if a teacher could take what he or she hears in a short workshop or two and go back to the classroom and implement it. Complicated ideas cannot be "taught" this way. Yet, the reality for most teachers is that a large portion of what passes for professional development has little connection to the context of their classrooms and the real dilemmas of practice they face. It rarely has systematic follow-up and support. And, in addition, it is most often an "add-on" in teacher's work lives.

What needs to be acknowledged is that teaching techniques are learned inside a school culture where adults are always seeking to learn more about their students and their craft. Educators need to develop the capacity to build such cultures. Teachers learn by inventing together and by understanding how to support one another.

A recent study of the California Subject Matter Projects, a statewide infrastructure for professional development, has shown how technical learning occurs within a supportive school culture (Stokes et al., 1998). Defining "site" as a place where a group of teachers is involved in a subject-matter project, the study produced an extensive list of characteristics that high quality sites and programs demonstrate (see Figure 4.2).

States, districts, schools, and teachers' unions all are involved in professional development, but many fail to connect the need to build pedagogical techniques and content learning with the importance of school-site follow-up and continuous support, reflection, discussion, and trial again. Without a culture of support, teachers find it hard to try things out, get feedback, make adjustments, and really integrate new ideas into their teaching.

Creating an Ethic of Collaboration

Although the new social realities for teachers include a movement away from being alone toward being a participating member of a community, accomplishing this change is no easy feat. Much of the time teachers are encouraged to learn alone but *act* as colleagues. Being colleagues and learning to work together in schools is a major and important innovation for teachers. They must deal with conflict, disagreements, and differences in a way that allows them to engage in common work. This is a skill that must be learned, and it requires many opportunities to work with one's colleagues (Bennis & Beiderman, 1997; Fullan, 1991; Hargreaves, 1994). It does not mean that everyone will always agree or things will always be "nice." But when teachers have opportunities to work, plan, and be together, they can achieve enhanced individual goals in their classrooms even as they are accomplishing collective ones for the school. In the words of one teacher:

> I have not only learned techniques for coping, but I am always with teachers who are passionate about their teaching. I was so excited and stimulated being part of the writing project that I came home every day with a headache. I found 24 others just like me! (Lieberman, Focus Group, 1998)

FIGURE 4.2

CHARACTERISTICS OF HIGH QUALITY SITES

- ◆ The opportunity for teachers to learn from other teachers
- ◆ The opportunity for inquiry and reflection
- ◆ The presence of generative structures (opportunities to invent)
- ◆ High quality disciplinary content
- ◆ The opportunity for direct engagement in *doing* the discipline
- ◆ The presence of professional practitioners of the discipline
- ◆ Coherence among different site components and activities
- ◆ The locus of programs as school-based and site-based
- ◆ The presence of multiple entry points into different site activities
- ◆ Multiple paths of continuing participation with the site
- ◆ Multiple ways for teachers to contribute to the work of the site
- ◆ A focus on serving targeted students, schools, districts
- ◆ The existence of collegial relationships among teachers
- ◆ The presence of active strategies for increasing the diversity of participants
- ◆ Symmetry between site culture and a vision for the classroom
- ◆ Deliberate attempts to design for maximum participation, inclusiveness
- ◆ The valuing of multiple sources of knowledge
- ◆ The valuing of reflection, debate, and intellectual discourse
- ◆ Proactive strategies to diversify site leadership

Source: Stokes et al., 1998, p. v.

There is no one way to accomplish this ethic of collaboration. It often starts with a few teachers who decide to do something together. There are many entry points for teachers to become colleagues. Doing something and learning from it is probably the most important way to start the process (Lieberman, 1995; see Figure 4.3).

TEACHER CAREER DEVELOPMENT AND PERSONAL CHANGE

Learning communities, supportive cultures, and an ethic of collaboration are all necessary for teacher development, but equally important is how teachers function as individuals. Too often, organizational roles

---

FIGURE 4.3

UNDERLYING PROCESSES OF TEACHER GROWTH

- ◆ Developing a professional community
- ◆ Combining inside knowledge and outside knowledge
- ◆ Creating an ethic of collaboration

---

and responsibilities are emphasized at the expense of individual concerns and needs. Teachers range in age from early twenties to mid or late sixties. Like the children they teach, they too pass through different developmental stages—from the trying on of new roles in early adulthood to the acceptance of one's mortality in mid and late adulthood. And, as in other developmental theories, these stages are not fixed; they are merely suggestive of general patterns. Each stage has its tasks and challenges; some are marked by balance and stability, while others are marked by crisis and disequilibrium (Erickson, 1950; Levinson, 1978). While men and women pass through similar life stages, they vary in the pace and intensity of the transitions. Childbearing and child rearing and care taking have special significance for women, though they are growing in importance to more and more men. Personal issues such as marriage, divorce, childbirth, change in economic status or needs, and care giving of children and aging parents affect the capacity of all teachers for commitment and growth.

Teachers also pass through a sequence of career stages that interact with their developmental stages. Fessler (1995) documents the interacting spheres that affect a teacher: (1) one's personal environment, which includes life stages, family, critical incidents, crises, individual dispositions, and avocational outlets; (2) factors in one's organizational environment such as unions, regulations, management style, public trust, societal expectations, and professional organizations; and (3) one's position in the career cycle, beginning with preservice education and moving on to induction, competency building, enthusiasm and growth, career stability, career wind-down, and exit. Michael Huberman's work (1995) focuses more extensively on the career cycle and chronicles a teaching career that has five stages. In years 1–3, teachers focus on issues of career entry, where survival and discovery are the major concerns. In years 4–6, teachers enter a stage of stabilization, followed in years 7–18 by two paths: one marked by experimentation and diversification and the other by stocktaking and interrogations. In years 19–30, teachers again follow one of two paths. Teachers who have been experimental move into serenity; teachers who chose stocktaking move toward conservatism. At the end of the career cycle, in years 31–40, teachers approach disengagement that can be either serene or bitter depending on previous paths and choices.

Yet another approach to individual teacher career development focuses on pedagogy (Academy for Educational Development, 1985). In early stages of their careers, teachers are preoccupied with the day-to-day problems of management, discipline, instruction, and subject matter. They struggle with the complexity of linking what they have learned to their work in practice. In the next stage, teachers learn the culture of the school and piece together an instructional program, a "personal survival kit" that helps them feel more confident but does not lead to personal inquiry. In the third stage, teachers reach a plateau of "generalized pedagogy." They are concerned with providing the best instruction for the most students. Finally, a small number of teachers progress to the stage of "differentiated pedagogy" where they discover fresh routes to effectiveness and consistently adapt instruction and curriculum to the needs, interests, and abilities of *all* students.

In order to link individual teacher growth to the school reform agenda, we need to understand some important variables: What accounts for individual growth and development from one stage to another? From less to more sophisticated pedagogy? From stabilization to experimentation and serenity rather than stocktaking and bitterness? Why do some teachers remain "stuck" while others progress? The research on individual teacher change provides some answers. One is posed by Susan Loucks-Horsley and Suzanne Stiegelbauer (1991), who reference more than two decades of evidence. They argue that personal concerns are pivotal to teachers' ability and willingness to adapt and change. When presented with an innovation, teachers pass through seven levels of concern: (1) Awareness (I am not concerned about it), (2) Information (I would like to know more about it), (3) Personal (How will using this affect me?), (4) Management (I seem to be spending all of my time getting materials ready), (5) Consequence (How is my use affecting kids? How can I refine it to have more impact?), (6) Collaboration (How can I relate what I am doing to what others are doing?), and (7) Refocusing (I have some ideas about something that would work even better). Loucks-Horsley and Stiegelbauer caution that "change is a process, not an event" and that teachers must adapt to change personally and developmentally (p. 17).

Another response to teacher change is offered by Beverly Showers, Bruce Joyce, and Bennett (1987), who conclude from their research that teachers need to have access to four conditions if they are to change.

First, they must *understand* the theory or reason behind any change they are asked to make or consider. Second, they must *see* demonstrations of the changed practice in a real classroom. Third, they must have *time* to practice the new behaviors associated with the change in an environment that honors and supports risk-taking. And fourth, they must have *opportunities for feedback* and *coaching* from colleagues and supervisors. If any of these conditions is not present, the authors argue, teacher change will not take hold, and teachers will retreat to old and familiar practices.

Yet another perspective on teacher change is offered by T. R. Guskey (1986), who challenges the conventional wisdom that a change in teacher beliefs and attitudes must precede any changes in teacher practice. Guskey's research supports just the opposite relationship. He argues that substantial change in teacher attitudes and beliefs occurs only after teachers have changed their practices and they begin to see the results of these changes in terms of student outcomes. This chain of events is explained, according to Guskey, by the intense relationship teachers have with their students and the connections they make between what they believe and what they see working in their own classrooms.

The literature on adult and teacher career development and the processes of teacher change supports the need to adapt professional development to the specific teachers for whom the development is intended. Every staff is a collection of individuals, each with his or her own personal and career history. One size does not fit all; this is as true for teachers as it is for the students they teach.

TRANSFORMING PROFESSIONAL DEVELOPMENT

As we examined the processes underlying teacher growth and teacher career development, we began to look more closely at what districts normally do when they spend their professional development money. Many districts choose a focus for the year (and many more change their focus every year). This means that teachers are often given the full menu of strategies for teaching literacy or the new standards in a particular subject matter. Our concern is not just that content is seen as a transportable basket to be "delivered" and then put into practice but also that adults are viewed as an undifferentiated group who all learn the same way and at the same pace. From our study of professional development, we offer three ways that it can be organized: direct teaching, in-school learning, and out-of-school learning.

Direct Teaching

Most professional development opportunities for teachers take the form of what we call "direct" teaching. These include workshops, presentations, and awareness sessions—all provided with the expectation that teachers will take the new ideas back to their classrooms and put them into practice. In numerous instances, teachers have told us that professional development opportunities are narrowly conceived and that their districts assume that direct teaching is the only way to provide new ideas for teachers. Teachers can be inspired through these methods, but they are often held captive to presenters who talk about new materials, strategies, and content without concern for implementation, adaptation, or feedback. Some districts routinely send teachers to conferences, provide courses and workshops, and hire consultants to help them implement new strategies for math, reading, science, or computing. This is all necessary, but it is not sufficient. At its best, it introduces teachers to new ideas and possibilities. At its worst, it makes faulty assumptions about the giving and receiving of knowledge and skills without paying attention to the need for practice, support, and feedback.

Learning in School

Much of what the current reforms call for, however, demands a different way of thinking, organizing, and supporting teachers (Lieberman, 1995; Little, 1993). For example, learning about literacy requires a very complicated set of skills, abilities, attitudes, strategies, and understandings. Teachers must try out new ideas, collect data to see what happens when they use those ideas, craft ways of responding to this information about their students, talk about the process with their peers and, most often, go back and try again using what they have learned.

Learning for teachers involves more than listening to ideas about school; it involves "learning *in* school" by trying out new ideas with peers and students as a regular part of the school day. There are many ways that teachers learn new ideas. Teachers learn by observing their students. They use a "running record" of how students read, they do a "descriptive review" of a student often who is having difficulty in class, or they collect data on how students do on a variety of assessments of their work. Teachers also learn by being observed by their peers and outsiders and receiving feedback on what they intended, what actually happened, and how the process looks from the outside. Classroom visits provide opportunities for teachers to explain to outsiders what they are doing in their school. When teachers are observed in these situations, the teaching and the learning processes are made public and thus are held up for shaping, understanding, and further development.

Teachers learn by working with others. They learn when they team teach as they discuss what and how they are going to work with students. They learn through teacher research groups as they make public their struggle to reach all children and to expand their repertoire by making themselves vulnerable as new learners (regardless of how long they have been teaching). Teachers learn when they write curriculum together, or when they work through the kind of standards they hold for their grade level, subject matter, or cluster. These kinds of learning often do not count for professional development, but they are the stuff of real learning in the context of one's work. Teachers also learn by mentoring others. Sharing their knowledge with new teachers causes them to sift through their years of stored up unexamined and unspoken experience—a process that helps them, as well as the new teachers—to organize their knowledge and gain insight into their own practice (Graham, Hudson-Ross, Adkins, McWhorter, & Stewart, in press).

Teachers learn when they think about, create, and use assessment measures, particularly when this involves them in figuring out with their peers what they believe in, what they disagree about, and eventually what they can agree on—as a community (Ancess & Darling-Hammond, 1994; Darling-Hammond & Falk, 1997; McLaughlin, 1998). Teachers learn when they pose problems that they have in their own classrooms and their work lives. In this way teachers have opportunities to pose a real question that they have, deal with something that they can change, collect evidence from their students, and interpret the evidence for further action (Cochran-Smith & Lytle, 1993).

As teachers learn in school they develop a language that encourages talk about student work and engages them in the creative task of joining their experience, their values, and their own growth as teachers. This is professional development of the highest order because it puts the task of teaching and learning in its rightful place—always evolving, deepening, expanding, learning from experience, and making that experience public, shared, and accessible to others.

Learning Out of School

Teachers also need to explore environments outside the boundaries and visions of their own schools. This is a form of outside knowledge. Educational reform networks and different styles of partnership offer opportunities for teachers to learn out of school (Lieberman, 1996; Miller & O'Shea, 1996). Networks (away from teachers' own schools) encourage trust, build support, and provide additional avenues for teacher learning. In building new cultures outside school, teachers often find themselves in groups (with other teachers and other people in their system who are not teachers) who have been brought together to reinvent, learn, and teach each other ways of working in school. These groups provide teachers with continual stimulation and ideas and put them in touch with colleagues who are working on similar problems of practice. Sometimes it seems easier to create groups outside one's school rather than inside, and to provide space for teachers to question, deal with seemingly intractable problems, and create and invent new solutions while gaining support from fellow strugglers.

In addition, educational reform networks give teachers opportunities to expand their repertoires and to become mentors, organizers, curriculum writers, and professional developers in their own right. These kinds of opportunities open up the world of education, writ large, to teachers who often feel constricted by the powerful, yet sheltered, nature of the classroom. When networks work well, they seem to allow teachers to weave their way through the tensions described above. They respect teachers' differences as adults and provide multiple ways for them to grow and learn. Teachers in networks assume new roles, become more confident in their own knowledge, and learn to teach what they know to others. Other institutions that are part of the network educate them too and broaden their perspectives and their experiences in what it means to be a teacher.

These networks and partnerships with colleagues are formed for different reasons by different groups and individuals, and they develop different histories (Lieberman & Grolnick, 1996). What makes networks and partnerships special to their members are the norms they create (e.g., being informal, having food, discussing their work over dinner), and the activities and relationships that encourage people to feel that they have had a significant part in shaping the work. Personal identification with and commitment to the network's purposes and to one's own learning in the context of a supportive community are the defining characteristics of successful networks.

A network is also a work of art to be crafted by the members as they continually negotiate the set of tensions that make the network especially responsive to its members. But networks are one more thing to belong to, another set of activities to go to, and an additional responsibility, and so to earn the loyalty and respect of teachers networks must deal successfully with these tensions. They must have a purpose that teachers can identify with and provide activities that are compelling enough to keep people coming. Sometimes the purposes of a network evolve and expand with the work, and sometimes groups seem to know that they have a big idea in need of constant shaping. Good networks and partnerships learn to negotiate between inside knowledge and outside knowledge. The League of Professional Schools, affiliated with the University of Georgia, asks that schools devise a school improvement plan, but before they go to work on it, the university provides them with a lot of material that will help them understand the full complexity of what they are undertaking. Sometimes a sponsoring university sets up the groups and provides the materials to be discussed, as with the well-known "dine and discuss" groups of the Southern Maine Partnership. But the important point is that school-based educators' knowledge, along with more generalized knowledge of research and reform, is seen as a critical part of the network. Networks find ways to govern that are more egalitarian than bureaucratic, providing a voice at the table for school-based educators who take part in shaping an agenda that confronts their school problems and allows for the members to teach each other what solutions might look like and to deal with any problems that are encountered along the way. Rather than formal workshops with no follow-up, good networks provide for formal, informal, evolving, and expanding agendas that develop as the network's members develop. This makes the network itself more developmental and less bureaucratic, more in keeping with its member's growth. And finally, networks must decide whom they are going to serve. Will it be teachers only, teachers and principals, districts? This decision is important because it affects the complexity of the work, the purposes, and the activities.

The purpose of this chapter is to emphasize that to meet the new social realities of teaching we must find new ways of providing growth-in-practice for teachers. It may not be easy, but we have many examples of how it can happen. If teachers are to make a commitment to lifelong learning, to becoming members of a professional community, to participating in reinventing themselves and their schools, they must be provided with organizational and individual experiences that carefully consider what these new realities demand. Most of us do not learn just by hearing a great lecture, but we can become inspired and excited by fresh ideas. For teachers this means organizational forms that provide for support and pressure, coupled with multiple entry points, sensitivity to teachers' career stages, and many opportunities to grow (see Figure 4.4).

FIGURE 4.4

ORGANIZING FOR PROFESSIONAL DEVELOPMENT

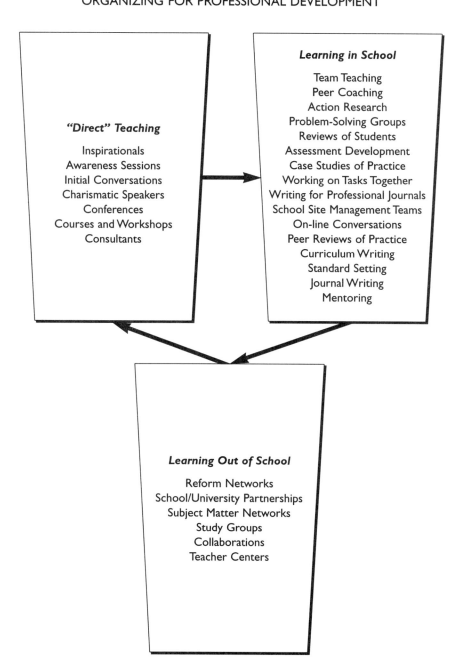

Learning in School

Team Teaching
Peer Coaching
Action Research
Problem-Solving Groups
Reviews of Students
Assessment Development
Case Studies of Practice
Working on Tasks Together
Writing for Professional Journals
School Site Management Teams
On-line Conversations
Peer Reviews of Practice
Curriculum Writing
Standard Setting
Journal Writing
Mentoring

"Direct" Teaching

Inspirationals
Awareness Sessions
Initial Conversations
Charismatic Speakers
Conferences
Courses and Workshops
Consultants

Learning Out of School

Reform Networks
School/University Partnerships
Subject Matter Networks
Study Groups
Collaborations
Teacher Centers

VIEWS FROM PRACTICE

Here we return to the four schools we discuss in Chapter 1. New Orchard Elementary School, Wright Middle School, Stratton High School, and Aronomink School all provide rich examples of learning in and out of school.

Learning in School

Formal research, informed inquiry, and personal or collective reflection of practices are much valued in these four schools. New Orchard and Aronomink have made teacher-led inquiry central to their work. At New Orchard, teachers have had grant support for two action research projects, one of which also involved parents as researchers. Today, New Orchard teachers are involved in a project that gathers extensive data on student achievement and uses these data to inform decision making. Aronomink has also used external funding to support teacher research. It began its restructuring efforts with a grant from the state to apply the notion of "school as a center of inquiry" to its work. Its teacher-scholar position is clearly identified and supports research as a critical element in the life of the school. Wednesday morning sharing sessions at Aronomink provide another way for teachers to reflect on their practice and on student work. At Wright Middle School, teachers spend considerable time collecting and analyzing data on student writing samples. They use these data to inform practice and to make recommendations for curriculum change. Stratton High School staff often refer to their school as "one grand seminar." Teachers are in the habit of holding their practice up to analysis. They use such reflective tools as the Tuning Protocol and Collaborative Assessment Conference to systematically look at and improve their practice. Finally, all four schools have developed structures that support and promote teacher inquiry and reflection. Regular release-time days, restructured faculty and team meetings, and summer institutes all provide time and opportunity for this work.

These four schools see student learning as the starting point and endpoint of teacher learning. Conversations are structured around students: what they know, what they do not know, what they need to know, and how they can demonstrate what they know. Teachers effectively use assessment of student work according to specific criteria of achievement as their principal way of focusing on learning. This process also helps refocus attention from what teachers do to what *students do.* For instance, New Orchard's benchmarking involves teachers in looking at student work on particular tasks in language arts and reading in second and fifth grade. Each work sample is scored by teachers who do not have the student in class, reinforcing the notion that it is what the student *does* that is important. Such close scrutiny gives the classroom teacher reliable information to use in constructing learning for the student. Aronomink's exhibition project in grade 3 serves the same purpose. Here, outside juries evaluate student performance. Also, at Aronomink, a thorough reading inventory is conducted annually on each student. The results are used by teachers to plan instruction.

At Wright and Stratton, the emphasis on student learning is just as pervasive, demonstrating that large middle and high schools can provide the same kind of individual attention that an elementary school does. Wright's Demonstration Fair is a culminating assessment that engages teachers and students as learners. Also at Wright, the "house plan" provides opportunities for teachers to examine student learning together. In addition, teachers use their in-house planning time to meet together to develop rubrics and scoring criteria that are the cornerstone of assessment work. At Stratton, joint teacher-student rubrics are used extensively in classrooms. A team system also supports personalization, with on-going discussions about assignments and projects, assessment criteria, and the quality of student work.

The four schools use structured protocols—the Collaborative Assessment Conference and the "Slice"—to guide their discussion of student work and their own teaching. The Collaborative Assessment Conference, developed by the Coalition of Essential Schools, is a highly structured process that engages a group of teachers in conversation about and analysis of student work samples. The conference begins with teachers reading or observing the work, which can be pictures, videos, writing samples, and so forth. The teachers then respond to a set of questions: What do you see in the work? What questions do you have about the work? What do you think this child was working on most ardently when making this product? Silent to this point, the teacher presenting the work is now invited to provide additional observations, to address the questions raised, and to describe the child at work on the piece. The conference then becomes a general discussion of what strategies the presenting teacher should pursue with the child and the rest of the class. The conversation might consider future assignments, responses to the child, content issues, and questions to explore. The conference ends with a review of the process and its effect on the participants.

The Slice is a way to obtain a cross sampling of student work. A representative group of students from the whole school is selected and everything these students create—homework, assessments, projects, worksheets, notes, drafts, videotapes—over one or two days is collected. Later, groups of teachers investigate the work, looking for trends and patterns. The Slice enables teachers to see whether and to what extent the principles they espouse are actually being enacted in their classrooms and throughout the school.

Both the Collaborative Assessment Conference and the Slice enable teachers to know their students well so they can develop classrooms that are learner-centered. Teachers at the four schools work from information that is collectively shared rather than from intuitions and impressions that are individually constructed. They use these data to develop strategies for instruction and to design particular interventions. More important, they have placed student learning at the center of the educational enterprise and made this "business as usual" in their schools.

Professional development within the four sample schools extends well beyond the traditional "make and take" workshops and direct instructional models that dominate elsewhere. It is intimate, immediate, and continuous. No longer viewed as a commodity that is delivered in disconnected segments during "in-service days" that are scattered across the academic year, it has become an integral part of teacher work. Teachers at the four schools have developed many tools they use for their own development. Among the most common and most promising are teacher research, collegial reviews of practice, curriculum work, and standards/assessment development.

Teacher research is a well-established tool in the four schools. Individually, or in small groups, teachers define a problem, gather data, analyze findings, and use the results to deepen understanding and improve practice. The "teacher scholar" position of Aronomink School is an example of one form of teacher research. Topics there have ranged from how students approach reading to how they use reflection to help them in their own learning. At New Orchard School, research has been conducted collectively on problems related to math and reading instruction, and on how students process emotional issues and the effect this has on learning. At Stratton High School, teachers researched student perceptions of de-tracking, and at Wright, there has been emergent research on the effects of keeping students with the same team of teachers over 2 years of middle school.

Collegial review of practice may take many forms. At root, these reviews are about the engagement of teachers in a critical and friendly analysis of their own practice. One of the strategies employed by Stratton High School is the "critical friends group," in which a trusted educator from outside the school leads groups of teachers in a reflection on their work inside the school. At Aronomink, the teachers take part in a series of "rounds," modeled on medical rounds, during which a small group of practitioners visits another in his or her classroom and afterward engages in a seminar aimed at identifying what went well and how things might have been done differently. A powerful tool that several of the schools have used is the "tuning protocol" for reflection on teacher work. It asks a teacher or team of teachers to present actual work (an assessment, a project, a unit, an idea) before a group of colleagues. The protocol has seven clearly defined and closely timed segments that move from presentation to critique to reflection. Central to the process is the idea of "warm" and "cool" feedback. Warm, supportive responses identify what is good in the work, while more objective, cool responses identify problems or what could be improved. Participants leave the tuning protocol with new insights about their own work and that of the presenter or presenters.

Curriculum work is another way that the faculties at the four schools engage in staff development as part of their daily work. It is considered a valuable way for teachers to learn and grow together. Each of the four schools has been involved in significant curriculum development. Stratton High School's entire program has been revamped; courses have been eliminated; new requirements have been implemented; ability grouping has been abolished. This has led teachers to develop new ways of giving "honors" credit to students, including implementing a system of differential assessments in *all* classes that allow students to choose whether they want to work toward "honors" status. Putting this system in place required hours of intense conversation about course outcomes within and across disciplinary lines. The conversations provided an opportunity for people to examine expectations, assess their beliefs and practices, and make changes in their approaches to teaching and learning.

At Wright Middle School, the whole staff has moved toward an expeditionary model of curriculum development. Within their teams, teachers develop interdisciplinary "expeditions" with a core set of outcomes, subject-specific activities, and an integrated project. For example, one of the houses developed a culinary expedition. The students designed and constructed a restaurant on site, developed print and nonprint materials, developed a menu and pricing procedures, designed management and service systems, and opened for business on two consecutive evenings. The teachers on the team, like those at Stratton, spent considerable time in conversation and planning activities. And as at Stratton, these conversations led to deeper understanding and changes in practice.

At the two elementary schools, curriculum work has been just as powerful a staff development approach. Both have moved toward multi-age, inclusive classrooms that require significant time and investment and learning for teachers. In addition, Aronomink School has collectively developed a template for designing interdisciplinary projects, and New Orchard has involved teachers in a long-range program of curriculum review and improvement. As at the high school and middle school, these curriculum activities not only led to improved experiences for children, they also led to increased learning for adults.

Learning in school is taken seriously at these four schools. They each make time during the school day and the school year for teachers to meet together, talk together, and work together. They use structured tools and protocols to facilitate the work. As a result, the teachers experience professional development as part of their daily lives in school. They look to each other and to their students as the source of their own growth, which is embedded in practice.

Learning Out of School

The four schools extend themselves beyond their boundaries, and in so doing honor learning out of school. They are all members of a regional school/university partnership, which has been in operation for 12 years. Through the partnership, they network with other educators, read and discuss articles and books over dinner, and engage in assessment and review activities. Aronomink and New Orchard were original members of the partnership and have been actively engaged in its activities since 1985. They were also active participants in an Early Childhood Education Group that met monthly for 4 years. In this group, principals and teachers read and discussed articles and books about the education of young children. The aim of the group was not to go back to schools and immediately implement new ideas. Instead, the group promoted the norm of critical inquiry and acknowledged the power of conversation and reflection. The teachers involved in the group developed a common language and a solid knowledge base as a springboard for action.

Wright and Stratton joined the partnership sometime later. Wright had already established itself as a middle school and was grappling with issues of appropriate curriculum when it became a member. It became one of three "demonstration" schools in the partnership to pilot a "planning backwards" model of assessment and learning over the course of 3 years. During that time, the Wright staff forged a close working relationship with a university faculty member. The result of this collaboration is the now annual Demonstration Fair. Stratton is a more recent member of the partnership. In a short time, however, the school became actively involved in partnership work and is now one of six high schools collaborating on ways to use the arts in student exhibitions of learning.

In addition to their partnership involvement, the four schools have developed independent affiliations with organizations beyond the region. Aronomink has long been associated with Project Zero at Harvard University and was one of four schools involved in the ATLAS Communications Project funded by the New Schools Development Corporation. New Orchard is an active member of John Goodlad's Network of Educational Reform and partners with a research and development group working on a data-driven system of change. Wright Middle School is a member of the Expeditionary Learning Project, another New Schools Development Corporation project, and regularly connects with that organization in unit design and implementation. Stratton High School is a member of the Coalition of Essential Schools and is now involved with other local schools in an Annenberg Rural Challenge Grant project. These local, regional, and national affiliations keep people from "getting stuck." They provide arenas for discovery and growth and opportunities for teachers to expand their horizons. When teachers move beyond their own school and connect with educators of like mind in distant places, they acknowledge the power of outside knowledge. This complements the inside knowledge they gain as members of their school communities.

TOWARD AN ERA OF HOPE, PASSION, AND COMMITMENT

◆ ◆ ◆ ◆ ◆

Know that many personal troubles cannot be solved merely as troubles, but must be understood in terms of public issues—and in terms of the problems of history making. Know that the human meaning of public issues must be revealed by relating them to personal troubles . . . . Know that problems of social science, when adequately formulated, must include troubles and issues, both biography and history, and the range of their intricate relations.

C. Wright Mills, *The Sociological Imagination*, 1959

SINCE 1984 when we wrote *Teachers: Their World and Their Work*, much has happened in the world and in schools. Many naive assumptions about changing schools have been tried, tested, and found wanting. The ways by which school bureaucracies have managed to alienate and silence students, parents, and teachers are deeply rooted in the regularities of the everyday life of schools (Lieberman, 1998; Sarason, 1996). This book illuminates the work that some teachers and principals are doing to replace these regularities with new social realities of teaching and learning. We have seen how, in the process of change, all parties become actively involved with the emotional and intellectual commitments of learning and teaching.

We, like many others, believe that we are in the midst of a public school crisis. There is certainly a crisis of resources. Many states and localities have systematically reduced the amount of money spent to support education, while making tremendous demands on schools and teachers to produce results and make comprehensive change. Although the demands are understandable, there must be adequate supports to make change possible. Too much pressure without attendant supports is creating massive shortages of teachers in some areas of the country and eroding the sense of hope that schools need in order to work effectively.

But there is another crisis, a crisis of ignorance. This crisis encourages irresponsible criticism and teacher blame. Panaceas abound. There are charter schools, teacher exams, privatizing schools, phonics, standards, assessments, a national voucher project, and comprehensive school reform models, to name a few. The mood is often mean and impatient, leaving teachers, who should be at the center of reform efforts, feeling marginalized, discouraged, and frustrated. This assault on teachers, their abilities, and intentions is in contradiction to the evidence we have witnessed and described. Teachers who take on the tough work of creating or recreating schools do so with a tremendous sense of *hope* (that all students can achieve success in school), *passion* (in their regard for continuously learning how to get it right), and *commitment* (to transforming teaching as they transform themselves and their schools). Not only are they heroes in their own schools, but they are helping others understand the practices, policies, and possibilities for creating democratic schools.

We are learning how to meet the demand for change by developing the supporting conditions that promote hope and commitment in teachers. This is not a romantic view of schools or teaching; it is based on abundant evidence that teachers have both an intellectual and a personal investment in their students. It is further supported by "existence proof" (Elmore, 1996), in the form of real-life examples, that by attending to people, processes, and content, we can develop meaningful and comprehensive school reform.

THE FUNDAMENTALS OF SCHOOL IMPROVEMENT

In our earlier work, we synthesized what we called the "fundamentals of school improvement," gleaned from research, craft, and intuition. These fundamentals were based on what we knew at that time and included:

- ◆ Working *with* people rather than working *on* them
- ◆ Recognizing the complexity and craft nature of the teacher's work
- ◆ Understanding that there are unique cultural differences in each school and that these affect both where school improvement efforts begin and what form they will take

- Building collaboration and cooperation involves the provision for people doing things together, talking together, sharing concerns, and building group norms over time
- Starting where the people are, not where you are
- Caring for people first and techniques second
- Making private knowledge public and being sensitive to the effects of isolation and trial-and-error learning on teachers
- Resisting simplistic solutions to complex problems and getting comfortable with reworking, finding enhanced understanding and enlightenment in the process
- Appreciating that there are many variations of school and professional development efforts and acknowledging that there is no one way to solve problems
- Using knowledge as a mode of helping people grow rather than pointing to their deficits
- Supporting improvement efforts by protecting ideas, providing time, announcing expectations, and making provisions for necessary resources
- Sharing leadership functions with a team so that people can provide complementary skills and get experience in role taking
- Organizing school improvement activities around a focus
- Understanding that successful improvement efforts have content that is salient but must also have a process or a structure to go with it
- Being sensitive to and aware of the differences between the worlds of the teacher and of the principal, understanding that they share a part of the work—time, climate of the school, and the possibility for group cohesion—but also acknowledging the demands on each that they do not share

NEW UNDERSTANDINGS ABOUT TRANSFORMING TEACHING AND SCHOOLING

Our understandings have become more nuanced, sophisticated, and detailed over time. Important new conceptions have helped us see how to support teachers in their efforts to transform themselves and their schools and how to see life in schools from their perspective (Cochran-Smith & Lytle, 1993; Hargreaves & Fullan, 1992; Lieberman, 1995; Little, 1993; McLaughlin, 1998). We'd like to propose eight new understandings to add to those we developed previously in 1984.

Creating a Seamless Web of Values, Practices, and Organizational Supports

Schools can organize in many different ways, improve the professional lives of teachers and expand their roles, challenge regulations, and remove boundaries, but if student learning and engagement are not the focus they will accomplish little of value for students. School change and improvement must focus on students. This is not simply a gimmick that will lead to an understanding of what the school stands for. This is what helps shape the values and beliefs of a school community. In fact, it is what builds commitment to a real learning community—a community that is shaped by its members' struggle to make a vision real.

Adopting programs or practices without understanding the consequences of given ideas, the assumptions underlying the work, and the organizational conditions necessary to make them happen, will inevitably breed cynicism and confusion (Giacquinta, 1998). Values without the necessary practices to help make them real make people feel like frauds. People learn by doing something, and when they take the time to reflect on what they are learning, they often become clearer about what they know, what they need to know, and what they believe (Schön, 1995; Weick, 1979). Too often goals and mission statements do not become grounded in practice and, thus, may inhibit or block real learning from taking place.

In the four sample schools we describe in earlier chapters, teachers constantly reviewed what they were doing to confirm that it was consistent with their beliefs and to determine what they needed to do to improve their efforts. They used their own feeling of discomfort and uneasiness and the comments that came out in public discussion of students' work to test whether the community was practicing what it believed and whether teachers felt supported. It became apparent that values, practices, and organizational supports are all connected. Values without continuous discussion of how they are put into practices will be as empty as bumper-sticker slogans. Practices that enact agreed-upon values that do not have organizational supports (time, meetings with agendas that focus on what students are accomplishing, teacher leadership, and continuous follow-up and feedback) will thwart rather than support teacher work and student improvement. Whatever the catalyst for school improvement, for change to be meaningful, values, practices, and organizational supports must be integrated.

Making Professional Development Integral to School Life

A significant shift is taking place in the understanding and practice of professional development. There is movement away from simply offering workshops and "telling" to knowing, understanding, acting, and reflecting, or what we call "growth in practice." Standard district days are being rethought. People are attending to what it means to learn on the job and be supported in the process, with discussion of what is being taught as well as what is being learned. While there is always the possibility that staff development will fall prey to the press to "adopt" school reform models and will be viewed as the new "silver bullet," we are encouraged by the direction that many schools are taking. The teachers and leaders we have described know that reform ideas, effective workshops, and district staff development must have structures, supports, time, facilitation, and continuous discussion *in their schools,* along with continuously developing practices, publicly discussed and worked on in the classroom and at team, grade, and department levels. They know that a focus on student work shifts thinking about their own development in an important way. Looking at student work through the lens of subject matter content helps teachers observe more carefully what students are learning, where they are having problems, and what other strategies might be more effective. Inquiring about student work keeps the discussion centered on students and makes collaborative discussions among teachers readily attainable.

Transforming schools and teachers demonstrate how professional opportunities are created and sustained. Different configurations that are invented to ensure that teacher learning takes place "inside" their school (using inside knowledge that teachers create), while they make use of "outside" knowledge (knowledge that stems from research, state standards, curriculum projects, reform efforts, and new forms of assessment) makes staff development, not just a set of strategies or workshops, but a way of focusing the collective work of teachers on their work with students. In the process professional development is taking on a new meaning. Like the necessary connections between values, practices, and organizational supports, professional development becomes a part of school life. *Structures* (new roles, relationships, mechanisms), *processes* (conversations, inquiry groups, standard setting, curriculum and assessment writing), and *support* (time, leadership responsibilities, and a variety of opportunities to learn) become the necessary components of continuous growth and development as part of rather than an addition to school life.

Supporting Teacher Learning Outside of School

Integrating professional development into the life of the school is a necessary condition for teacher learning. But equally important is learning outside of school. Teachers thrive by taking materials from outside sources such as speakers and networks and using and practicing them inside. The importance of combining inside and outside work cannot be underestimated. Inside problems can be discussed with outside people who are themselves struggling with the same kinds of problems. Networks and partnerships, when they are successful, provide a safe and trusting set of relationships with people undergoing the change process. What must ultimately be the work of teachers in their own schools and classrooms is supported by "outside" friends who share similar expectations.

Sometimes outside networks, partnerships, or friends can serve as a constant reminder of ultimate purposes or high expectations that often get lost in the confusion of the day-to-work of effecting change in a school—even when things are going well. Networks are important because they identify with the common struggle. They do not have to provide close, intense relationships; their strength is in the "weak ties" that bind them together (Granovetter, 1973). In this way outsiders can support, encourage, and empathize, but they can also teach, model, provide a supportive pressure, and add dignity to the struggle to get better. Networks and outside partners can serve as organizational friends who are there when needed, who can provide opportunities for role taking, cross-role grouping, collaborating, and knowledge sharing—all important supports for change. When whole schools join partnerships or networks, an outside group can help speed the process of what goes on inside a school. But the work that eventually matters must take place inside the classroom and the school.

Leading and Learning as a Collective Responsibility

Schools and teachers who take on the challenge of working toward positive changes for their students inevitably face the changing nature of leadership in their schools. Neither principals nor teachers can lead on their own; they need each other. And they need to learn new skills and habits along the way. Principals struggle with when to step in, when to facilitate, when to let others make the decisions and the mistakes, when to provide for practice or when to start all over again. They become diagnosticians, assessing their communities to figure out the best entry points for change, keeping track of both social and intellectual needs, providing opportunities for discussion, allowing conflict to become more open, and accommodating differences among teachers. At the same time, teacher leaders have to figure out how to hold themselves accountable, while making sure they have all the necessary materials, supports, and authority to be responsible. Their leadership may be subtle and inconspicuous or it may be overt and very much out in the open.

None of the principals we observed took total responsibility for being instructional leaders, not because they could not, but because building a community of shared interests and shared responsibilities meant that all participants in the change effort were taking responsibility as community members. Learning skills of collaboration, openness, and clarity is difficult work for everyone. Building trust, protecting ideas, and establishing new norms of caring and concern for one another as well as for students takes time, effort, and capacity. They are the glue that holds a professional community together.

Maintaining Balance

There are always contradictions and tensions in the work of school reform. It is necessary to assume a balance—between content and process, teacher and student needs, action and reflection, pressure and support, responsibility and accountability. The content of the curriculum has been a source of contentious struggle throughout the history of public education (Goodson, 1998). It should not be surprising that the curriculum wars are being enacted once again. Curricular content alone will not make a difference in student learning; there must be a process that makes teacher learning important, focused, and continuously supported. We have observed that schools that press content without a process for discussion, action, and reflection make superficial and cosmetic changes that do not last. Nor can lasting changes be made when the effort focuses endlessly on process discussions. Finding the balance is the key to organizing for change.

Balance is also necessary in terms of teacher and student needs. Professional relationships, new ideas, expanded strategies for student learning—all need time and mechanisms appropriate to the context of each school. Again, too much focus on teachers can improve their lot and not necessarily improve the learning of students; and too much focus on students, without paying attention to teachers' learning environments will inevitably lead to frustration and anxiety. No matter where successful schools start to change, they inevitably strike a balance between teacher and student needs—encompassing both in their work.

Action and reflection also demand a balanced perspective. Like their students, teachers need to actively engage in trying out new ideas and then have time by themselves, and eventually with others, to think about what happened, learn from it, and try it again. Too much action without thinking about its results and too much study and reflection without action will both meet the same fate—cynicism and a sense of defeat among the participants. The combination of doing something in the classroom and also of having opportunities to think, talk, and analyze what went on is critical to those who actually transform their schools.

In addition, schools need to balance pressure and support. The public and political clamor for good schools is exerting great pressure on teachers. This is understandable in the light of the changing social conditions that make it critical that schools meet the needs of all students. However, pressure without the necessary supportive, organizational, and learning conditions to help make changes possible will inevitably fail (Sarason, 1990). As we point out above, "growth in practice" strategies that are coupled with continuous pressure engage teachers in conversation, clarify expectations, and promote practices that make serious school change possible.

Finally, accountability needs to be balanced with responsibility. When teachers are convinced that they will be supported and that their needs are taken seriously, they will take responsibility for making changes in their teaching. Pressing accountability measures, such as higher test scores, without supporting teachers in their quest to accomplish all that they can do for their students is misguided. What the public wants for its children must be provided for the adults as well. The press for test scores unrelated to the need for learning in the entire community will ultimately lead to greater frustration for the public and its schools. Schools that are transforming find ways to address the pent-up frustration that many parents feel toward their schools and to provide the kinds of supportive conditions teachers need to answer the concerns of parents with more effective practice. Balancing responsibility and accountability helps satisfy all constituencies simultaneously.

Establishing Conditions that Support the New Social Realities of Teaching

At the center of school change is the ability and capacity of principals and teachers to make the transition from isolated schools to schools that offer a rich and supportive environment for students and adults.

This happens with different points of entry and on different schedules. Change is characterized by the collective involvement of teachers in goals for the school that become larger than their own personal goals for their classroom. It happens as teachers get involved in collective struggles about student learning and engagement—rather than those that remain solely internal or private. It happens when student work can be discussed with colleagues rather than judged in isolation using one's intuition as a guide. It happens when teachers willingly engage in learning outside as well as inside their school and talk about it with their colleagues. It happens when a level of trust is sustained over a long period of time. It happens when the community recognizes that learning is not a one-time thing but is recursive, often stressful and challenging before it is rewarding. It happens when teachers struggle openly with a need to identify with their school or team or grade level but at the same time not give up their own sense of identity and strong feelings about being a teacher. It happens as teachers incorporate expanded strategies for student learning into their own repertoire and feel comfortable enough to talk about it, learn from it, and in some cases, teach it to others.

Making the transition from isolated schools to learning communities means that principals and teachers become involved in a change effort that is characterized by evolutionary planning that leaves room for shaping and honing ideas. Sometimes, it is necessary to go back to the beginning when plans go awry or when detours veer too far off the track. It is often hard to include everyone, when some people constantly put up roadblocks. In the end, however, acceptance of differences and patience are better strategies than isolation and derision.

Learning About and Understanding the Change Process

We have more knowledge about change efforts than we have ever had before. This knowledge comes from scholarship (Fullan & Hargreaves, 1996; Hargreaves, Lieberman, Fullan, & Hopkins, 1998) as well as from tales from the field—close observations of teachers and principals involved in building professional communities in their schools. These tales demonstrate how practices unfold that give shape to values and mission statements. They teach how ideas propel action and how reflection helps clarify beliefs. They reinforce the lesson that teachers have to *experience* learning with their students in order to really change their practice, and they show that experience is long term before it is internalized.

As teachers learn new practices and habits of mind, they experience the uncertainty and ambivalence that inevitably accompany new learning. Organizational learning and personal learning are not the same. Collegiality is more complex than previously portrayed. The development of a culture of colleagueship has a change process of its own. Tensions sometimes arise over how to negotiate being together and being alone (Hargreaves, 1994). Teachers have to do things in their own classroom first before they are comfortable sharing it with their peers. They need to talk to each other before they are comfortable watching each other. When the topics of conversation are about the work that students produce and the strategies that teachers use, the talk is most meaningful. Learning opportunities for teachers are best if they are not just episodic. Annual shifts in focus do not provide the time necessary for significant and important learning to occur. The more that learning opportunities are built into a larger framework for change, the more professional development becomes an integral part of the school. What counts for professional learning becomes substantively changed. Teachers read material on reform and then they make it their own as they shape new knowledge to fit the context of their work. Packaged learning becomes inappropriate; inquiry becomes the major form of professional growth that leads to change.

The process of change is never smooth, rational, or linear. When things do not go well in schools that are transforming, they develop the courage to regroup, plan again, and find ways out of the confusion. Despite conflict, which sometimes seems ubiquitous, teachers learn how to make it productive—rather than destructive. Sometimes it takes external help to teach people how to talk to one another in such a way that the work, rather than interpersonal differences, can go forward. Having many perspectives is critical to school and teacher transformation. Different perspectives may produce tension, but it is the kind of tension that needs to be understood and worked through. When teachers pull in the same direction, they nurture each other's passion for teaching students and their commitments to each other.

Protecting and Nurturing Hope, Passion, and Commitment

When teachers work together to transform themselves and their schools, they rediscover why they came into teaching in the first place and why they have persisted. They demonstrate that with adequate resources, both human and material, realities do change. These resources are often obvious; they include time, a variety of opportunities to learn, assistance with teaching strategies, equipment and materials, a principal who is also learning about how to facilitate schools as communities, a shared and collective vision about what the school believes, and a district that supports school change with autonomy as well as responsibility and accountability for itself as well as for its schools.

What is not so obvious is the need for protecting budding ideas, welcoming new learnings, and supporting teachers by looking for and celebrating successes. The fragmentation of learning is just as harmful for adults as it is for students. Going too fast, throwing out too many ideas at once, not providing time for practice or reflection, making faulty assumptions about adult learning, creating leadership roles without providing opportunities to learn how to enact these roles—all this leads to failure and despair.

Teachers and their students occupy a special, but sheltered, existence. Being with students all day is both exhilarating and exhausting for teachers; it gives them insights not known or seen by other adults. Such intimacy and knowledge bestows power, but it also builds in a dependence on students for emotional and intellectual sustenance. In isolated settings, teachers may become wary of other adults and fail to see them as sources of support and learning. Transforming teachers in transforming schools are learning to do just the opposite. They are learning that adult communities are critical for their own growth and development and that professional communities are their richest source of support. Such communities keep hope alive and provide the energy and compassion that all people need as they engage in change. They meet needs that are rarely met by bureaucratic solutions or by edicts to change that emanate from sources far away from where students and teachers live.

Perhaps the greatest lesson we have learned from our study of teachers and schools in the midst of change is that a new view of teaching and community is being crafted, one that takes place not only inside classrooms and schools but outside as well, one that respects diversity and confronts differences, that represents a sensitivity to and engagement with the whole life of students as they live it. The creation of new learning communities that include rather than exclude, that create knowledge rather than merely apply it, and that offer both challenge and support provide the greatest hope for teachers who are in the process of transforming themselves, their world, and their work.

REFERENCES

Academy for Educational Development. (1985). Improving pedagogy: Phases of teacher development. In *Teacher development in schools* (pp. 21–31). New York: Ford Foundation.

Ancess, J. (1998, April). *The reciprocal influence of teacher learning, teaching practice, school restructuring, and student learning outcomes.* Paper presented at the meeting of the American Educational Research Association, San Diego, CA.

Ancess, J., & Darling-Hammond, L. (1994). *Authentic teaching, learning, and assessment with new English-language learners at International High School.* New York: National Center for Restructuring Education, Schools, and Teaching.

Banks, J. (1992). Creating multicultural learner-centered schools. In *Building learner-centered schools.* New York. National Center for Restructuring Education, Schools, and Teaching.

Battistich, V. D., Solomon, D., Kim, D., Watson, M., & Schaps, E. (1995). Schools as communities, poverty levels of student populations, and students' attitudes, motives, and performance: A multilevel analysis. *American Educational Research Journal, 32*(3), 627–658.

Bennis, W., & Biederman, P. W. (1997). *Organizing genius: The secrets of creative collaboration.* Menlo Park, CA: Addison-Wesley.

Boyer, E. (1991). *Ready to learn: A mandate for the nation.* Princeton, NJ: Carnegie Foundation for the Advancement of Teaching.

Brown, A. (1994). The advancement of learning. *Educational Researcher, 23*(8), 4.

Clark, D. L., & Meloy, J. M. (1990). Recanting bureaucracy: A democratic structure for leadership in schools. In A. Lieberman (Ed.), *Creating collaborative cultures: Building the future now* (pp. 3–23). Philadelphia: Falmer Press.

Cochran-Smith, M., & Lytle, S. L. (1993). *Inside/outside: Teacher research and teacher knowledge.* New York: Teachers College Press.

Darling-Hammond, L. (1990). Achieving our goals: Superficial or structural reforms? *Phi Delta Kappan, 78*(4), 286–295.

Darling-Hammond, L., & Falk, B. (1997). *Using standards and assessments to support student learning: Alternatives to grade retention.* New York: National Center for Restructuring Education, Schools and Teaching.

Darling-Hammond, L., & McLaughlin, M. W. (1995). Policies that support professional development in an era of reform. *Kappan, 76*(8), 597–604.

Delpit, L. (1995). *Other people's children: Cultural conflicts in the classroom* (pp. 21–47). New York: The New Press.

Dewey, J. (1980). Democracy and education. In Boydston, J. (Ed.), *John Dewey: The middle works 1899–1924.* Carbondale: Southern Illinois University Press. (Original work published in 1916.)

Dewey, J. (1985). Democracy and education. In Boydston, J. (Ed.). *John Dewey: The middle works 1899–1924.* Carbondale: Southern Illinois University Press. (Original work published in 1929).

Elmore, R. (1996). *Staff development and instructional improvement: Community District 2, New York City.* Paper commissioned by the National Commission on Teaching and America's Future.

Elmore, R., & McLaughlin, M. (1988). *Steady work: Policy, practice, and the reform of American education.* Santa Monica, CA: RAND Corporation.

Erikson, E. (1950). *Childhood and society.* New York: Norton.

Fessler, R. (1995). The dynamics of teacher career stages. In T. R. Guskey & M. Huberman (Eds.), *Professional development in education: New paradigms and practices* (pp. 171–192). New York: Teachers College Press.

Fullan, M. (1991). *The new meaning of educational change.* New York: Teachers College Press.

Fullan, M., & Hargreaves, A. (1996). *What's worth fighting for in your school?* Toronto, Ontario: Public Schools Teacher Federation.

Garcia, E. (1991). *The education of linguistically and culturally diverse students: Effective instructional practices.* Santa Cruz, CA: National Center for Research on Cultural Diversity and Second Language Learning.

Giacquinta. (1998). Seduced and abandoned: Some lasting conclusions about planned change from Cambire School. In A. Lieberman (Ed.), *Roots of educational change in the* International Handbook of Educational Change, Part One (pp. 163–180). Dordrecht: The Netherlands: Kluwer Academic Publishers.

Goodlad, J. (1984). *A place called school.* New York: McGraw-Hill Book Co.

Goodlad, J. (1988). School-university partnerships for educational renewal: Rationale and concepts. In K. Sirotnik & J. Goodlad (Eds.), *School-university partnerships in action: concepts, cases, and concerns* (pp. 3–31). New York: Teachers College Press.

Goodson. (1998). Patterns of curriculum change. In A. Lieberman (Ed.), *Roots of educational change in the* International Handbook of Educational Change, Part One (pp. 231–241). Dordrecht: The Netherlands: Kluwer Academic Publishers.

Graham, P., Hudson-Ross, S., Adkins, C., McWhorter, P., & Stewart, J. M. (In press). *Teacher/mentor: A dialogue for collaborative learning.* New York: Teachers College Press.

Granovetter, M. S. (1973). The strength of weak ties. *American Journal of Sociology, 78*(6), 1360–1380.

Guskey, T. R. (1986). Staff development and the process of teacher change. *Educational Researcher, 15*(5), 5–12.

Hargreaves, A. (1994). *Changing teachers, changing times: Teachers work and culture in the postmodern age.* New York: Teachers College Press.

Hargreaves, A., & Fullan, M. (1992). *Understanding teacher development.* London: Cassell.

Hargreaves, A., Lieberman, A., Fullan, M., & Hopkins, D. (1998). *International handbook of educational change, Volumes One and Two.* Dordrecht: The Netherlands: Kluwer Academic Publishers.

Houston, H. (1988). *Building a professional culture in schools.* New York: Teachers College Press.

Huberman, M. (1995). Professional careers and professional development: Some intersections. In T. R. Guskey & M. Huberman, M. (Eds.), *Professional development in education: New paradigms and practices* (pp. 193–224). New York: Teachers College Press.

Levin, H. (1991). *Expanding democracy through schooling.* Paper presented at the Seven Oaks Symposium.

Levinson, D. (1978). *The seasons of a man's life.* New York: Knopf.

Lezotte, L., et al. (1980). *School learning, climate and student achievement.* East Lansing: Michigan State University, Center for Urban Affairs.

Lieberman, A. (1995). Practices that support teacher development: Transforming conceptions of professional learning. *Phi Delta Kappan, 76*(8), 591–596.

Lieberman, A. (Ed.). (1995). *The work of restructuring schools: Building from the ground up.* New York: Teachers College Press.

Lieberman, A. (1996). Creating intentional learning communities. *Educational Leadership, 54*(3), 51–55.

Lieberman, A. (1998). The growth of educational change as a field of study: Understanding its roots and branches. In A. Hargreaves, A. Lieberman, M. Fullan, & D. Hopkins (Eds.), *International handbook of educational change* (pp. 13–20). Dordrecht: The Netherlands: Kluwer Academic Publishers.

Lieberman, A., Falk, B., & Alexander, L. (1994). *A culture in the making: Leadership in learner-centered schools.* New York: National Center for Restructuring Education, Schools, and Teaching.

Lieberman, A., & Grolnick, M. (1996). Networks and reform in American education. *Teachers College Record 98*(1), 7–45.

Lieberman, A., & McLaughlin, M. W. (1992). Networks for educational change: Powerful and problematic. *Phi Delta Kappan, 73*(9), 673–677.

Lieberman, A., & Miller, L. (1984). *Teachers: Their world and their work.* New York: Teachers College Press.

Lieberman, A., & Miller, L. (1988). School improvement in the United States: Nuances and numbers. *Qualitative Studies in Education 1,* 3–19.

Little, J. W. (1981). *School success in staff development: The role of staff development in urban desegregated schools.* Boulder, CO: Center for Action Research.

Little, J. W. (1993). *Teachers professional development in a climate of reform.* New York: National Center for Restructuring Education, Schools, and Teaching.

Little, J. W. (1996, month). *Organizing schools for teacher learning.* Paper presented to the American Educational Research Association Invitational Conference on Teacher Development and Reform, Chicago.

Lortie, D. (1975). *Schoolteacher.* Chicago: University of Chicago Press.

Loucks-Horsley, S., & Stiegelbauer, S. (1991). Using knowledge of change to guide staff development. In A. Lieberman & L. Miller (Eds.), *Staff development for education in the '90s: New demands, new realities, new perspectives.* New York: Teachers College Press.

McDonald, J. (1991). *Dilemmas of planning backwards.* Providence, RI: Coalition of Essential Schools.

McLaughlin, M. W. (1998). Listening and learning from the field: Tales of policy implementation and situated practice. In A. Hargreaves, A. Lieberman, M. Fullan, & D. Hopkins (Eds.), *International handbook of educational change* (Pt. 1, pp. 70–84). Dordrecht: The Netherlands: Kluwer Academic Publishers.

McLaughlin, M. W., & Oberman, I. (Eds.). (1996). *Teacher learning: New policies, new practices.* New York: Teachers College Press.

McLaughlin, M. W., & Talbert, J. (1993). *Contexts that matter for teaching and learning.* Stanford, CA: Stanford University, Context Center on Secondary School Teaching.

Miller, L., & O'Shea, C. (1996). School-university partnership: Getting broader, getting deeper. In McLaughlin, M., & Oberman, I. (Eds.), *Teacher learning: New politics, new practices* (pp. 161–184). New York: Teachers College Press.

National Commission on Excellence and Education. (1983). *A nation at risk: The imperative of educational reform.* Washington, DC: U.S. Department of Education.

National Commission on Teaching and America's Future. (1996). *What matters most: Teaching for America's future.* New York: Teachers College Press.

Newmann, F. M., & Wehlage, G. G. (1995). *Successful school restructuring.* Madison: Center on Organization and Restructuring of Schools, University of Wisconsin–Madison.

Resnick, L. B. (1987). *Education and learning to think.* Washington, DC: National Academy Press.

Richert, A. (1991). Using teacher cases for reflection and enhanced understanding. In Lieberman, A., & Miller, L. (Eds.), *Staff development for education in the nineties* (2nd ed.). New York: Teachers College Press.

Rosenholtz, J. (1989). *Teachers workplace.* New York: Longman.

Rutter, M., Maughan, B., Mortimer, P., Ouston, J., & Smith, A. (1979). *Fifteen thousand hours.* Cambridge: Harvard University Press.

Sarason, S. (1990). *The predictable failure of school reform.* New York: Teachers College Press.

Sarason, S. (1996). *The predictable failure of educational reform.* New York: Teachers College Press.

Schaps, E., Watson, M., & Lewis, C. (1996). A sense of community is key to effectiveness in fostering character education. *Journal of Staff Development, 17*(2), 42–47.

Schlechty, P. (1988). Schools for the twenty-first century: The conditions for invention. In Lieberman, A. (Ed.), *Building a professional culture in schools* (pp. 233–255). New York: Teachers College Press.

Schlechty, P. (1990). *Schools for the 21st century.* San Francisco: Jossey Bass.

Schön, D. A. (1995, November/December). The new scholarship requires a new epistemology. *Change, 27*(6), 27–34.

Sergiovanni, T. (1987). The theoretical basis for cultural leadership. In Sheine, L. T., & Schoenheit, M. B. (Eds.), *Leadership: Examining the elusive* (pp. 116–130). Alexandria, VA: Association for Supervision and Curriculum Development.

Showers, B., Joyce, B., & Bennett, B. (1987). Synthesis of research on staff development: A framework for future study and a state-of-the-art analysis. *Educational Leadership, 45*(3), 77–87.

Shulman, J., Lotan, R., & Whitcomb, J. A. (Eds.). (1998). *Groupwork in diverse classrooms: A casebook for educators.* New York: Teachers College Press.

Shulman, L. S. (1993, November/December). Teaching as community property. *Change, 25*(6), 6–7.

Sizer, T. (1984). *Horace's compromise.* Boston: Houghton Mifflin.

Stokes, L., Caskey, N., Heenan, B., Hirabayashi, J., Medina, K., Ramage, K., & St. John, M. (1998, February). *Evaluating professional development: An exploration of the quality and (qualities) of the California Subject Matter Projects* (Report No. 15). Inverness, CA: Inverness Research Associates.

Stokes, L., Sato, N., McLaughlin, M. W., & Talbert, J. (1997). *Theory-based reform and the problem of change: Contexts that matter for teachers' learning as community.* Stanford, CA: Center for Research on the Context of Teaching, Stanford University.

Task Force on Teaching as a Profession. (1986). *A nation prepared: Teachers for the twenty-first century.* New York: Carnegie Forum on Education and the Economy.

U.S. Bureau of Education. (1917). *The money value of education.* Washington, DC.

Weick, K. (1979). *The social psychology of organizing* (2nd ed.). Reading, MA: Addison-Wesley.

Whitehead, A. N. (1929). *The aims of education and other essays.* New York: Macmillan.

INDEX

The letter *f* after a number indicates a figure.

ABOUT THE AUTHORS

Ann Lieberman is an emeritus professor from Teachers College, Columbia University. She is now a Senior Scholar at The Carnegie Foundation for the Advancement of Teaching and a Visiting Professor at Stanford University. She was president of the American Educational Research Association (AERA) in 1992. She is widely known for her work in the areas of teacher leadership and development, collaborative research, networks and school–university partnerships, and increasingly, in the problems and prospects for creating learner-centered schools. Her books and articles on teacher development and school change are numerous and have been influential in turning the field toward a more expanded view of what counts for teacher learning. Her recent books include *Building a Professional Culture in Schools, Staff Development for Education in the '90s: New Demands, New Realities, New Perspectives* (with Lynne Miller), and *The Work of Restructuring Schools*.

Lynne Miller (B.A., University of Pennsylvania; MAT, Harvard University; EdD., University of Massachusetts) is Executive Director of the Southern Maine Partnership and Professor of Educational Leadership at the University of Southern Maine. The Partnership now includes thirty-three school districts, the University of Southern Maine, Southern Maine Technical College, and the Maine College of Art. Closely aligned with the University's Extended Teacher Education Program, which Lynne directed for its first three years, the Partnership seeks to combine teacher and school development through opportunities for conversation, action, and reflection among educators from the southern third of the state. Lynne has written widely in the fields of teacher development and school reform. In addition to numerous articles and papers, she has completed three other books with Ann Lieberman. She served as member of the National Commission on Teaching and America's Future and is now on the steering committee overseeing the implementation of the Commission's recommendations in the State of Maine. In addition, she serves on the state's Professional Development Design Team and works closely with the state professional organizations.